Celebrating ·

the Southern Seasons

Rituals for Aotearoa

First published in 1995
by Tandem Press
2 Rugby Road
Birkenhead
North Shore City
New Zealand

ISBN 0 908884 54 0

Illustrations by Juliet Batten
Design and production by Jacinda Torrance/Paradigm
Cover circle by Juliet Batten
Cover photograph by Mark Adams

Printed in Hong Kong by Kings Time

Celebrating the Southern Seasons

Rituals for Aotearoa

Juliet Batten

TANDEM PRESS

And what are the seasons of the years save your own thoughts changing? Spring is an awakening in your breast, and summer but a recognition of your own fruitfulness. Is not autumn the ancient in you singing a lullaby to that which is still a child in your being? And what, I ask you, is winter save sleep big with the dreams of all the other seasons.

Khalil Gibran, *The Garden of the Prophet*

Dedication

I dedicate this book

to the mountain Taranaki whose inspiring cone
overlooked my childhood.

to the river, Waionganaiti, which flowed
through the early years of my life.

to Te Henga, the place of healing,
inspiration and refuge for me in my adult years.

to my forebears: in Yorkshire on my mother's side;
in Ireland, Wales, Scotland and France on my father's side.

to my Celtic ancestors.

to my ancestors of old Europe, the gods and
goddesses, and especially to the Great Goddess herself,
who has held and nurtured me in my creative work.

I also pay tribute to my teachers

Sandy Ingerman, shaman, from the Michael Harner Institute,
who introduced me to shamanic journeying.

Rupert Sheldrake, whose theory of morphic fields gives
credence to so much that is felt and known in the bones.

Luisa Teish, for her gutsy, loving approach to ritual.

Jean Houston, for her inspirational work across cultural
boundaries, which has given me the courage to do this book.

to the many kuia and kaumatua who have shared their
Maoritanga with such generosity over the years.

And finally, to my dear sisters in my ritual group,
Cone, who continue to journey with me into new realms.

Juliet Batten

My thanks to the many people who have believed in this book, and given me support. Wayne England, Shirley Temm, Rosemary Arnoux, Mufridah Ulmansky and Aroha Yates-Smith helped me locate source material. Mary Hancock, Helen Palmer, Jill McLaren, Rosemary Arnoux, Peter Hubbard and Bronwen Nicholson read the text at various stages and made useful comments. Mary Hancock's mix of affirmation and challenge was particularly valuable. Dell Wihongi, Te Rarawa, was there from the start, giving me encouragement and the gift of her time and knowledge. She, Ruth Tai, Tuhoe, and Te Warena Taua, Kawerau-a-Maki, all read the finished text and gave helpful feedback and support. Bradford Haami and Mere Roberts freely shared with me their impressive research on the kiore. Graeme Murdoch, whose knowledge spans Maori and Celtic cultures, was generous with both his time, reading the text at different stages, and his wisdom, pointing me to additional material, and offering much that has enriched this book.

E iti noa ana taku, na te aroha.
(Though my present be small, my love goes with it.)

Contents

Preface   9

Introduction   13

The meeting-point   15

Seasonal celebrations and the nature of ritual   22

Seasonal rituals for Aotearoa   34

WINTER SOLSTICE   35

Aotearoa   36

Pagan Europe   44

Christian Europe: Christmas   51

Rituals for today   54

FIRST LIGHT   59

Aotearoa   61

Pagan Europe   63

Christian Europe: Candlemas   66

Rituals for today   69

SPRING EQUINOX   73

Aotearoa   74

Pagan Europe   82

Christian Europe: Easter   85

Rituals for today   86

FLOWERING AND SAP-RISE   90

Aotearoa   92

Pagan Europe   95

Christian Europe: May Day   99

Rituals for today   103

SUMMER SOLSTICE 107
Aotearoa 108
Pagan Europe 114
Christian Europe: St John's Day 117
Rituals for today 119

FIRST FRUITS/LEAN TIME 124
Aotearoa 125
Pagan Europe 131
Christian Europe: Lammas 133
Rituals for today 135

AUTUMN EQUINOX 138
Aotearoa 140
Pagan Europe 145
Christian Europe: harvest 149
Rituals for today 151

LAST LIGHT 154
Aotearoa 155
Pagan Europe 162
Christian Europe: All Souls, All Saints,
All Hallows Eve, Halloween 165
Rituals for today 169

Seasonal rituals for the year: summary 174

Celtic traditions and cosmology 176

Maori traditions and cosmology 184

Songs and chants for the seasons 195

Bibliography 200

Index 206

Preface

It is summer solstice, December 1993, and I am sitting on a beach of golden sand watching the sunrise. Some friends are with me. We have formed a circle around a red cloth, on which are placed summer fruits: strawberries, pineapple, mangoes. Above us the branches of a pohutu-kawa tree stretch out, with bristling crimson blossom reaching up to the sky. Bees buzz in the nectar-filled flowers.

We have met for ritual. Using sea water, we wash away the year, with all its tensions and burdens. One woman dips her hands in the bowl, leaving them there for a long time. Another flicks water all over her face, and another wets her forehead. We then take time to celebrate the achievements of our year, each using a symbol that she has brought as a point of focus. We name our hopes for the new cycle. We link hands and meditate and draw strength from each other. The sun rises on this longest day, and as we watch it we know this is the turning point towards darkness.

I return to the city strengthened and refreshed, grounded and connected with the cycle of the year. Later that day, as I do my shopping I hear the jangle of Christmas music, see all the trappings of a European Christmas and enjoy the thought that I will celebrate it in June, at winter solstice. I remember the pohutukawa and the beach and ground myself once more in this land, and this season.

What is a ritual and why do we do it? My book *Power from Within* addresses these questions in depth and gives guidelines for those who wish to develop their experience with ritual. As the book points out, we do rituals all the time, whether we are conscious of it or not. At the simplest level, a ritual is a symbolic act that carries an extra layer of meaning. It is often repeated, maybe daily, weekly, annually, or according to the occasion. The difference between a ritual and a habit is the degree of attentiveness we bring to it: if I grab my dinner and watch it in front of television, I am simply eating dinner. If I set the table with care, placing flowers and candles on it, and invite my friends to link hands for a moment's silence or thanksgiving before the meal, then my intention goes beyond eating dinner. It is about coming into

relationship, welcoming my friends, and offering them my attention and love.

Ritual often has a higher intention, which lifts us out of the mundane level of our lives. In ritual we connect with greater energies that have the power to sustain and inspire us on very deep levels. Ritual allows us to make transitions mindfully, from the small, such as greeting someone with a handshake, to more elaborate rituals of encounter, such as those of the marae, and the major transitions of life and death. Rituals may be private, shared with a special person, such as the wedding anniversary dinner, or shared with the community, such as the office farewell or the laying of a foundation-stone in a new building.

The seasonal round brings about its own shifts and transitions and since ancient times people have held rituals to mark these.

When I published *Power from Within* people wrote to me from all over the country, telling me how important they had found this book. Many of these people lived in remote rural areas and were quite naturally tuning in to seasonal changes and marking them in some way, often very simply. As I subsequently travelled about the country teaching ritual workshops I became aware of a growing number of people who seek to deepen their connection with the land, the seasons, the key moments of the life cycle and also with each other. Ritualising their experience in the context of community is one way of doing this.

I was constantly asked for more information about seasonal traditions, and realised it was time for another book. My work had grown out of an urge to reclaim the feminine spiritual traditions, and in doing so I had found inspiration in the practices of old Europe, especially as they survived in the Celtic traditions and the practice of Wicca. (Wicca comes from Anglo-Saxon, meaning 'to bend or shape', and was the name for the covens that met in early Christian times to preserve the old ways of the Goddess.) In researching further for seasonal celebrations I returned to these traditions in which the feminine principle was revered and the whole cycle of life celebrated. They provide the foundation for my own ritual practice as a member of the ritual group, Cone, as well as the public rituals I have been involved in over the last decade.

However, I was mindful that even though the pagan rituals may still resonate deeply in Pakeha consciousness, they are not the traditions that grew out of this land. It was necessary to inquire into the indigenous practices and to ask what the attitude was of the ancient Maori to the seasonal cycles of Aotearoa. What was happening in the bush, sea and cultivation fields? And how did people respond to these seasonal events?

A further question then evolved. What is the relevance of these practices, both of European and Pacific origin, here today in this country? To answer this I have gone to the land, to see how it speaks to us of seasonal change. I have gone to contemporary society, to look at how we organise our working year and economic structure. And I have gone to the meeting-point, that edge where the two cultures[1] touch, and discovered both surprising correlations and telling discrepancies. All of this has gone into the melting pot out of which I have drawn suggestions for contemporary rituals. They are suggestions only: some people will prefer to use the information to enhance ritual practice within their own culture, but others may wish to hold an awareness of the other stream that flows to the meeting-point in this land today.

Unfortunately, the seasonal celebrations of Aotearoa/New Zealand society today bear little relationship to what happens here in the natural world. British colonisers imported the Roman calendar without any adjustment to the fact that Aotearoa/New Zealand is a Southern Hemisphere island in the Pacific Ocean. Because of this a serious dislocation has taken place and each of the celebrations has been severed from its roots in seasonal activity. For example, Christmas originally grew out of pagan Yule, the winter solstice festival that took place on the longest night of the year. It made sense then to feast and make merry, but not now that it is associated with summer solstice, the longest day of the year, when we are preparing for summer holidays. Easter was an old spring festival, timed for that moment when all of nature is quickening, hens are laying, rabbits and hares are mating, and vegetation is greening. It made sense to celebrate resurrection from the dead then, but what sense does it make to do this, as we now do, in autumn? Again, Halloween has been imported from the United States of America, where it takes place in October, in late autumn; but it was not translated to fit the Southern Hemisphere, and so we cele-

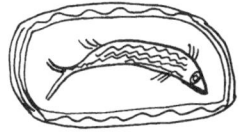

brate this festival of the dead at a time when nature is springing into life. This kind of incongruence both illustrates and ensures our alienation from the natural world and our ability to identify with it.

Celebrating the Southern Seasons offers a new opportunity: first to become aware of the customs, symbols, stories and meanings relating to seasonal changes from both European and Maori perspectives; and secondly for us to respond creatively to this knowledge as we celebrate and make our rituals today.

It is my hope that in the sacred space of ritual it will be possible for the different spiritual traditions to meet; that we will be held by a deep love and respect for this land, for each other, and for the heights and depths of human consciousness.

Juliet Batten, 1995

1. Although there are, of course, other cultures in Aotearoa today, this book focuses on the indigenous Maori and the colonising European cultures, which constitute the meeting-point of greatest impact on our history.

Introduction

The book begins with a chapter entitled 'The meeting-point', and goes on to give an overview on seasonal celebrations, the nature of ritual and the importance of place. Suggestions are given on how to structure seasonal rituals for individuals, families and community groups.

A calendar is then offered for Aotearoa. The next eight chapters follow the seasonal calendar, which is arrived at by taking the main divisions of the solstices and equinoxes, and the times mid-way between. These comprise the eight main festivals in the wheel of the European year. The Maori year followed a lunar month system that recognised the solstices, and like early Celtic society often observed a festival on the first new moon following the seasonal signal. Overlaying all this is the official calendar we follow today, that of the Christianised Romans, who conquered the Celts. Although the Romans killed and suppressed the Druid priesthood, they did not succeed in destroying the seasonal festivals; rather they took the course of attaching the Christian celebrations to the old pagan ones. This process was sometimes aided by a resonance between the seasonal practices in both cultures, and sometimes was done very consciously as a political strategy. An important proponent of this was the Roman bishop St Augustine, who arrived in Kent with 40 monks in AD 597 to convert the latest arrivals of a century earlier, the Anglo-Saxons. In time a gradual shift took place, resulting in Christian practices underlain with pagan associations: scratch the surface on any of our current festivals and the old pagan ways soon reveal themselves.

Each seasonal section examines the heritage from Maori, pagan European and Christian traditions and ends with suggestions for seasonal rituals in Aotearoa today. They are suggestions only, intended to stimulate more ideas on the part of the reader. I hope that the information I have collected will help people to form their own synthesis, and to enjoy working creatively with their ritual practice, while respecting the principles of the traditions they are drawing from.

The final section offers an overview of both Celtic and Maori traditions and cosmologies. It should be noted that both traditions

were diverse, and differed from one tribal area to the next. In both cases also it is largely by historical accident that the material has come down to us, depending on who was in a certain place at a certain time. Celtic and Maori spiritual traditions were oral, and the first written accounts were inevitably those of the colonisers: the Romans in Celtic Britain, the Pakeha in Aotearoa. Wherever possible I have checked out this material with the holders of the living traditions – through literature and film with the Celts, and through personal contact with representatives of different Maori iwi.

The most accessible source of information on early Maori practices comes from the Tuhoe people on the east coast of the North Island, via the work of Elsdon Best, but I have tried wherever possible to draw on other sources. The seasonal information for Aotearoa, like the rituals practised by different tribes, naturally varies from one district to the next. I hope readers will feel free to make their own observations of what is happening in their district, and adjust accordingly. Variations in dialect have been preserved in the Maori quotations.

The meeting-point

Where is the meeting-point for Maori and Pakeha today? Where is the ground on which we can stand and dialogue, bring the gift of our differences, and exchange the richness of our various cultural heritages? Within Maori society, the marae traditionally provided the space for differences to be ritualised, disputes to be settled, and visions shaped; that sacred ground where the power of the ancestors is invoked and people may speak from the heart, knowing that space is made for them to be heard. People claim this sacred ground when they know who they are: their tribe, their mountain, their river. The marae then becomes their turangawaewae (place to stand).

For some Pakeha (and Maori as well), their sacred ground has been that of the Church. For many, the Church has been abandoned and their sacred ground is less easily defined. Some Pakeha have become privileged visitors in the Maori world by virtue of their capacity to immerse themselves in Maoritanga and because they have been so generously included by the tangata whenua. Some are able to claim their own heritage with pride; others feel the effects of a history of cultural dislocation; and those who have arrived more recently may still feel like manuhiri (visitors). There are Pakeha who feel strong in their own spiritual traditions and others who feel that their ground of spiritual belief has been disjointed, or tainted with the oppressive practices of colonial Christianity. While some Pakeha are able to bring their own spiritual strength to the meeting-point, others tap the hollow vessel of their own spiritual vacuum when they encounter the richness of Maori ritual.

On the marae, while some Pakeha bring a knowledge of Maori protocol and language that enables them to meet the tangata whenua with dignity, others shuffle from foot to foot, embarrassed at their failure to respond adequately to the soul greeting of the tangata whenua. Some flinch at the thought of claiming their ancestry, when they know that their forebears ravaged the forests, ripped off the people, killed and cheated, creating a society where rift valleys of inequality still cut deep.

To bring respect for Maori culture and the capacity to meet Maori people from within their own cultural practice is one way to approach the meeting-point. However, it does not address the question of what it is we bring as Pakeha. We need to bring more than just material culture to the meeting-point, for we face a people whose spiritual traditions and rituals are vibrant with life. What would happen if we took courage and faced our ancestry, tracing it back through the events of a colonising history, to where we can draw on the richness of our past? If we traced it back to spiritual practices that were about power from within, rather than power over? If we lived in respectful relationship with the land rather than holding dominion over it?

For some, it might mean going back to the roots of Christianity and the values taught by Christ. For others, it might mean going back even further, to their cultural roots in Celtic and Old Europe, when people lived in close partnership with the land and ritualised their experiences of its changing aspects. For these people, the rhythms of life were deeply embedded in their consciousness, and were expressed in seasonal rituals.

Modern city-dwellers tend to be less in touch with rhythm-consciousness; often it is women, aware of the power of their menstrual cycles, who articulate the value of it today, leading to claims that rhythm-consciousness is gender-specific. Of course this is untrue: it has always been available to those who are in touch with the rhythms of their own life cycle, who watch the skies, observe the tides, or live and work on the land. Such was the case for the Celts as well as their forebears in the neolithic societies of Old Europe who were the first farmers. They revered the rhythmic throb of life and the power of the feminine, as embodied in the Great Goddess.

The Great Goddess was the creator, nurturer and destroyer of all life, holder of the Blood Mysteries and the cycle of birth, death and renewal. She was one with the life-force that flowed through springs and wells, the sun, moon and stars, and the moist, fertile earth. She was associated with animals, birds and fish. Later she gave rise to the many goddesses of Europe: Athena, Hera, Artemis and Hecate in Greece; Minerva and Diana in Rome; the Morrigan and Brigid in Ireland; Laima and Ragana in the Baltic.[1]

Her symbols flowed over houses, vases, figurines and wall paint-
ings: meanders and zigzags depicting life-giving waters, moon and sun
symbols, eggs, birds and fish. Creatures of transformation such as the
butterfly or snake reflected the transformative powers of the Goddess
herself. In the figurines she appeared as the Great Mother enthroned,
giving birth, full-bodied and redolent with life; or as the Lady of the
Birds, Lady of the Beasts, the Living Waters or Goddess of the
Underworld. Sometimes she was accompanied by her power animals,
such as the leopard or horned bull. Sometimes her face became bird-
like and her arms became wings, or she took on the aspect of a reptile.

Rhythm-consciousness was reflected in the seasonal rituals in honour of the Goddess or her son/lover. Time was first measured by the
moon, whose phases were linked with the menstrual and life cycles of
women. The waxing moon represented the Maiden, associated with
the colour white. The full moon was the Mother, associated with the
colour red. The waning moon was the Hag or Crone, who was both
wise woman and seer, associated with death and the colour black. The
Goddess herself went through these phases with the seasons of the
year, ageing into the Hag in autumn and winter, birthing herself as
Maiden in spring and growing into the Mother in summer.

As agriculture developed the Goddess became the Grain Mother
who sacrificed her maiden daughter at harvest. In mourning she with-
drew her energy from the earth, and all nature went through a period
of dying. Then in spring the Maiden returned from the underworld and
the Grain Mother rejoiced, with the whole earth bursting into life. She
is best known today as Greek Demeter, mother of Persephone.

The male was originally associated with hunting as the Horned
God. Later he became Lord of the Grain, associated with the greening
of vegetation and the cycle of the sun. At winter solstice he was born
as the Sun King, the divine child of light, who grew to maturity until
the spring festival, later called Beltane by the Celts. This was when the
sacred marriage with the Goddess, as the Maiden returned from the
underworld, took place. Summer solstice was the moment of consummation, when the Sun King's energies were at their peak. It was also
the moment of death, for at this time the sun loses power. At harvest
the Sun King was felled with the grain, destroyed by the Goddess who

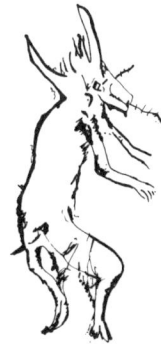

was both his mother and lover. He was taken into her dark womb, where he lay through the autumn festival later known by the Celts as Samhain, until winter solstice, when he was born once more as the divine child of light. The male god is re-emerging in our time, as the Green Man, the one who expresses the spirit of the ever-changing cycle of vegetation on the planet.

Rhythm-consciousness lived on in the rituals of subsequent European cultures thousands of years later. The story of the Celts is one example. Originally an élite tribe of Aryan origins, they went through a gradual change as they moved into Europe, assimilating many of the values of the old neolithic cultures as they settled various parts of the continent, moving on into the British Isles in around 500 BCE. The ancient Goddess cultures were particularly influential in the Basque Country, Brittany, Ireland and Wales, all areas occupied by the Celts.

Celtic rituals around the seasons honoured the triple goddess in her phases of spring Maiden, summer Mother and autumn Crone, as in neolithic times. In the male cycle, the young vegetation god or divine Sun Child followed the ancient pattern of birth, death and rebirth, with spring Beltane and autumn Samhain being key festivals. Samhain was when people brought their cattle in for winter shelter, and Beltane when the cattle were released once more to green pastures.

These rhythms dance in counterpoint to those of the Maori, whose ancestors spent thousands of years in the islands of the Pacific after journeying there from mainland Asia. In Maori society the year was divided into two phases: the winter months when hunting and gathering took place mainly in the bush, and the summer months when emphasis shifted to the sea. Whereas for the Celts it was the cattle that moved from one seasonal location to another, for the Maori it was the iwi (tribe) or hapu (sub-tribe) that moved, depending on whether food was to be gathered from the seacoast or the inland bush. At the same time, the rhythms of Maori life were closely linked with the kumara cycle, with its spring planting, autumn harvest and winter storage. These rhythms also mirror those of European agricultural societies that cultivated grain.

Much of the Celtic imagery is resonant with that of Maori spirituality; for example, the sacredness of the colours red, white and black, and the spirals that densely twisted and turned throughout their art work. The head was the sacred container of the soul, being severed from enemies and placed on gateposts or in doorway niches. History was oral, and as in Maori society the Celts developed memories that could retain vast genealogies, myths and history. Celtic time was reckoned in nights, not days, and the nights of the moon were all named and deemed auspicious or not, just as for the Maori. Night-time was feared by both Celts and Maori, for this was when the faeries were afoot and it was best for people to stay inside. The constellation of the Pleiades was an important marker of the seasons for both Maori and Celts, and in both cultures the land was revered, together with sacred trees and waters. Song and chanting were a powerful form of expression for the Celts, and their bards were famous.[2]

It is exciting to discover these similarities, but we do not have to be alike in order to meet. Our differences are just as significant. For example, the Celtic calendar of seasons revolved around the practices of cattle-rearing and, later, grain-growing. There is the importance to the Celts of the four powers or elements: earth, water, fire and air, each of which was associated with a particular compass direction, time of day, season and symbol. And there is the distinctively Celtic character of the gods and goddesses, who, like those of the Greeks and Romans, had their own stories and roles in the life of the people.

The Celts were colonised, first by the invading Anglo-Saxons in the fifth century BCE, and later by the Romans, who brought Christianity with them and did their best to stamp out Celtic religion. However, it continued to reverberate through the layering of Christian festivals and still remains available to us if we are willing to reach for it.

By the time Europeans had colonised Aotearoa in the 19th century, some had lost touch with the old ways, being city-dwellers practising a religion that frowned on a pagan relationship with land and seasons. When they arrived here, the final loss occurred. The seasons ceased to match up, and many of the new arrivals, daunted no doubt by the overwhelming task of surviving in an alien land, simply imposed their European concepts upon it. They were unable to respond to what was here, and continued to practise their European festivals without

consultation or self-reflection. While there were always those who responded with extraordinary openness and respect to the people and the environment of Aotearoa, for others land became a commodity to be bought, stolen or seized, and any sense of the land as sacred was left far behind in the distant past of race memory. These people have left a legacy of oppression and exploitation that can easily overshadow the genuine attempts of many to sustain practices based on integrity and respect.

How can we remedy this? Valiant efforts are being made by some to find partnership at the level of economic, social and political life. At times it seems the wounding is too great, the dislocation too severe. In order to gain more solid ground, we may need to address the spiritual level as well.

This means finding our own place of spiritual belonging here, and discovering just what that means for us. It might be about daring to belong and daring to connect with the spirit of this land. It might be about bringing our spiritual heritage with us, in a way that is empowering and allows the heart to open to others. When as Pakeha we claim our sacred place, our spiritual connection with the land, we enter into partnership with both the land and its people. Then we can bring our love, courage and vision for the future. We are more likely to care for the earth and want to heal it, no matter how great a task this may seem. We are more likely to hear, to see, to meet Maori people, and to face the task of healing the rifts between us.

We might find in ourselves a place of deep respect – for the land and all its people, past, present and future. Those who have gone before have created a layer of spiritual connection and intimate relationship with the taonga that is Aotearoa. But it is about even more than respecting the land and the indigenous culture. We can also bring our knowledge and sense of connection, the spiritual knowing that still sings along our bones, and bring another layer to what is already here. By reclaiming our own spiritual heritage we bring a gift. We might bring our ancient traditions and rituals, based around cattle-rearing and grain-growing, to the practices of our present economy. We might bring our traditional songs and dances as an offering of ourselves. We might acknowledge the meaning in the plants, foods, songs and stories that we have brought: to reclaim the sacredness of the oak, the hazel, the dandelion, the hawthorn and the holly; to offer the story of the Corn Mother and her lost daughter Persephone with the loaf of bread, to bring the Green Man to meet Tane, god of the forest, the Great Mother to Papatuanuku, the seven goddesses of the Pleiades to the 'little eyes' of Matariki, the Celtic goddess Brigid to Mahuika, and Hecate to Hine-nui-te-po. We might draw on the past in order to develop new rituals which we can share with others. While we discover the connecting points between our cultures, we can also claim and honour the differences.

In this way an exchange takes place. We who have taken so much, begin to give. We meet at the sacred place of ritual, the meeting-point. The roots of the oak touch the roots of the pohutukawa in sacred soil. We nourish our connection; we nourish our respect. And from here, action arises; we may begin the healing that makes partnership possible.

Seasonal celebrations
and the nature of ritual

Ritual marks transitions, beginnings and endings. It helps us catch up with ourselves. On the simplest level, spring-cleaning or gathering in the firewood are rituals that make us mindful of the changing seasons. Some people put away their summer clothes at the onset of the cold season, an action that expresses acceptance that the warm days are indeed over. Bottling fruit and haymaking are seasonal rituals based on storing goodness for lean times ahead.

Celebrating the seasons is as old as the hills. To celebrate the seasons is to join with the cycles of life: as the movements of the sun and moon bring changes to the face of the earth, so do the movements of our own lives bring changes and transitions.

Today, although many of us live in cities, the movements of the seasons are constantly with us. Just think of how often we listen to the weather forecast, and how remarks on the weather are embedded in our greeting rituals. Fashion houses greet each season with gusto, releasing their new spring or autumn collection. The changeovers from netball to tennis, rugby to cricket, or the opening of the yachting season, all get our attention.

And much of our experience resonates with the seasons. In spring the blood quickens, there is often a new energy for life, and we are more ready to initiate new ventures. In winter we often go inward: not only literally, staying at home more, but also within ourselves. We face our fears, and are more likely to get sick. It is a time for reflection, very different from the outgoing energy and renewed health that comes with summer. Heightening our awareness of the seasons through ritual allows us to honour our own rhythms and cycles. We remember that we are not static beings whose lives move in linear fashion, but that we are held by the wisdom of the circularity of life.

Seasonal rituals connect us with the energies of each phase of the year and allow us either to celebrate or to mourn the passing of one phase into the other. The ritual allows us to leave something behind and to embrace the new, to live in the present moment rather than drag our heels in the past. For people in a grieving process, a new season may mark the end of a phase and the opportunity to move forward. The holiday season that follows summer solstice is an occasion for shedding the old year, often through the rituals of office parties, and going into a phase of renewal.

On a deeper level still, seasonal rituals may connect us with a reverence for life, for the mysteries of the natural world, and for the great power of the universe, whether we call it God, the Goddess, or the life-force.

> There is a season, turn, turn, turn,
> And a time for every purpose under heaven.

The importance of place

A sense of sacred place was important to both Maori and Celts. In Maori culture a tuahu (place of ritual) might be located at a puna (spring) or wai tapu (sacred water). The tuahu could be a natural feature, such as a rock outcrop, but was usually a small structure made of a heap of stones with one or two stones set upright in the earth, or it consisted of a pou (post) set into tapu ground. Sometimes tuahu were used to ascertain the angle of the sun and stars for planting and other seasonal purposes. The elements of earth, water and fire were all significant. Kokowai or karamea (red ochre) was also associated with ritual, as were natural features such as rocks and especially trees, still important to various tribes today.[3]

Trees were also important to the Celts, each tribe having its own sacred tree. The Celts held rituals in sacred groves, the Druid priests especially favouring groves where the magical mistletoe grew on oak trees. Wells, springs and other sacred waters offered significant places for ritual. To the Celts, the association of a sacred tree with a well or spring added power to the location, for here the underworld and the heavens were connected. Stones from more ancient times often marked ritual places, and often an earthwork was formed, a small wooden structure built, or a sacred pole was set up.

When we make a place for ritual today we might consider these elements. We might create a special place in the garden for ritual purposes, placing there a special stone, planting a tree that changes with the seasons, such as a kowhai, kotukutuku or deciduous tree such as crab-apple, and if possible, bringing in water in the form of a fountain, bird-bath or pond. A brick or gravel path might be made to the place, and a sense of threshold created through planting, or marking with stones. The place might have a fire pit as a point of focus, and a circular pathway around it; or water or a tree could be the central point. Herbs might also be planted for fragrance and healing energies.

As a ritual place is used, it gathers power and becomes a sacred place, as if the earth and all the elements resonate with the energies gathered there.

Forms of ritual

Different ritual forms are possible depending on the spiritual traditions of the participants. In the Wiccan tradition (see *Power From Within*), we meet in a circle, with symbols placed in the centre. Maori people have their own forms, which are often based on lines of people, as is appropriate to rituals of encounter. Christians may prefer to use the altar as a focal point, placing symbols there and incorporating the various elements into the church service. This synthesis of Christian and pagan has taken place since the early centuries of Church worship, the harvest festival being a recent example.

The seven stages of ritual

When we are creating seasonal rituals, it may be helpful to be aware of the following seven stages:

1. PREPARATION
This may take many forms. On the physical level, it means getting the space ready, knowing what we are going to do, who will lead the ritual if there is to be a leader, gathering the symbols and any other

equipment that may be needed, and making sure there will be no interruptions.

On an energetic level, it means purifying any emotional or mental 'clutter' that might stop people from being fully present at the ritual. It means removing energies that do not belong. Cleansing with the use of water is the most common way of clearing energies and preparing for ritual.

In Maori rituals of encounter, preparation takes place as people wait, all together, before the kaikaranga calls them on to the marae.

2. ORIENTATION/OPENING/GROUNDING

We need to know why we are here, and to locate ourselves securely so that we can be open to the ritual. Orientation may simply occur when someone greets people and states the purpose. In Maori ritual, greetings and the concept of opening the space are important. The hongi, where noses are touched in greeting and the mauri or spiritual essence exchanged, is a vital part of orientation. Karakia (prayers) in honour of the ancestors and the place also play an important role.

In the Wiccan tradition that developed out of the practices of old Europe, sacred space is created by the 'casting of the circle', done through invocation or the linking of hands as people sit or stand in a circle. This gives the ritual its container. Next comes the honouring of the four directions with their associated elements, to allow orientation according to the direction of the sun and the hemisphere of the earth where the ritual takes place. In the Southern Hemisphere these are: south (earth), west (water), north (fire) and east (air).[4] Finally the centre, the meeting-point of all things, is named and honoured.

3. CENTRING

(This may be interchangeable with orientation.)

Holding hands and closing our eyes for a moment of silence is a simple way to centre. Singing a song or chanting is another way. Invocations that call in greater energies also help us to centre, often bringing about a change of consciousness.

4. ENACTMENT

This is the 'heart' of the ritual, when the central intention is carried out. On a marae, it may be when the speeches are made. In a Christmas ritual, enactment often consists of the handing out of presents, or the presentation of a nativity play. In a spring planting ritual, enactment is the placing of seeds in the earth. In a harvest ritual, it is the uplifting of the symbolic 'first fruits', or perhaps a breaking of bread baked from the first grains.

Enactment may be accompanied by song or dance, symbolic actions of various kinds, stories, prayers or blessings.

5. DEEPENING

This phase allows for the meaning of the enactment to be absorbed. The singing of waiata in Maori ritual is an example of deepening, for it opens up space and shifts levels, so that we take in what we have heard in a different way. Meditation and silence also allow for deepening to take place.

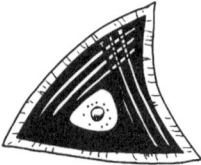

6. CLOSING

It is important to close the ritual formally, as often a special atmosphere has been evoked. People may have experienced quietness or a special opening in themselves, and need to know when to come back to everyday awareness. Closing may be done through simply stating that this is now the end, or with a formal blessing or prayer, or perhaps a song.

7. REINTEGRATION

This brings people back into the everyday world and is a bridging time. Sharing food and drink is the time-honoured way to reintegrate; with seasonal rituals, this is a perfect opportunity to enjoy seasonal foods. Rituals may be celebrated with just one or two people, in a family, or in a community group. Each of these rituals will have its own flavour, and there will be different ways of going about it.

Personal rituals

One or two people can be enough for a satisfying seasonal ritual. The advantage of having just one or two is that the ritual can be highly personalised, and your unique connection to the season expressed.

1. PREPARATION

Choose a quiet place where you will be uninterrupted. You may choose to make a sacred place in your own home, where you enact all your seasonal rituals. It is a good idea to make a small altar, and on it to place symbols for the season. You may choose a different-coloured altar cloth for each season, or burn a different-coloured candle each time. Instead of using an altar, you may arrange symbols on a special cloth placed on the floor. Before beginning the ritual, take the phone off the hook. In many traditions people shower or bath before a ritual, and put on special clothes so that they bring themselves fresh and open in a way that honours the sacred nature of ritual.

To prepare for the content of the ritual, you may wish to ask yourself the following questions:

• What does this season of the year mean to me?
What are the symbols, colours, smells, tastes and textures
that belong to this season?

• What is the quality or essence of this season?

• How does this quality or essence speak to me about
my own life now?

• What is it I wish to honour and hold to at this time?
How can I use the energies of this season to help me
let go of what is passing, and carry me forward into the new?
What symbolic act will express what I need to do?

2. ORIENTATION

Placing symbols in the directions of the south (earth), west (water), north (fire) and east (air) is a good way to begin. In the centre you place a candle, symbols for the season, or a symbol for the whole of life. You may wish to orient yourself with respect to your ancestors, your connection with the land, or with the phase of the moon, as well as the season you are celebrating.

3. CENTRING

Take time to be still, maybe closing your eyes, and breathe in the essence of the season. You may wish to hum or chant for a while, to gaze at the symbols you have brought, or even look into the flame of the candle – whatever helps to still your mind and tune you in.

4. ENACTMENT

This is the time for the symbolic action that will connect you to the season. You will already have prepared for this. If you are doing the ritual with someone else, be respectful of each other while each of you enacts their own part.

5. DEEPENING

Sit quietly and take time to absorb what has just happened. Be open to any way of expressing or simply registering this. Don't rush this process; take plenty of time. If you are alone, you may wish to draw or write in order to deepen your experience.

6. CLOSING

Give thanks for what has happened, blow out the candle and put away whatever has been finished with.

7. REINTEGRATION

Take time to eat and drink, in order to bring yourself back to everyday reality.

Family rituals

Children love ritual, and families that include ritual in their lives offer their children a great sense of enrichment as well as providing a lot of fun. Family rituals are best kept light and colourful, with simple actions that everyone can be involved in. The challenge is to find things that work for everyone, no matter what their age. This may mean finding activities that appeal to the child within us all, rather than expecting children to fit in with the adult world.

The best settings for a family ritual may be around the table, around a fire (either inside or outside), in the garden ritual place, or in the living room – whatever location is your gathering-place.

1. PREPARATION

Involve the children at this stage. They love anticipating an exciting event and will respond better if they have been drawn in from the start. If it is a winter solstice ritual, get them to make decorations for the tree, for example. If it is a spring planting ritual, let them choose the seeds they would like to plant, and help with the preparation of the seed dishes.

You may start incorporating ritual into your lives with something short and simple at the table, before the meal begins. In this case, make a centre-piece together, or build up a small altar in the centre by placing a cloth over a box or upside-down cake tin. Add some candles, and you have your sacred space.

Part of the preparation involves everyone washing their hands, and in doing so washing away any negative thoughts or feelings. It can be fun to do this together, and to name them: 'I'm washing away my crossness / my tiredness / being in a rush / my thoughts that rituals are silly.'

2. ORIENTATION

Everyone sits around the table. Maybe the four directions are named: south (earth), west (water), north (fire), east (air), and each child places their symbol for one of these directions in the appropriate place. The candles are lit and the purpose of the ritual named, for example: 'Today is spring equinox when the day and the night are exactly the same length. From now on the days will get longer and the nights will get shorter. We are going to celebrate this before we start our spring feast.'

3. CENTRING

This could happen by everyone holding hands and being silent for a few minutes, or singing a song together.

4. ENACTMENT

This can be quite short and simple, but something that children can feel part of. For example, at a spring equinox ritual each child might plant seeds into a dish and sprinkle them with water as they say a wish. Enactment may take place after the meal, and the meal used as a time for stories about the season, or for each person to have a turn at answering a simple question about themselves and the season: for example, 'What do you most look forward to now the days are going to get longer?' Enactment may take the form of a treasure hunt or a ritual journey of discovery. Be inventive.

5. DEEPENING

A song or a blessing may happen here. It could be a moment of silence, or may be held by saying, 'We are all going to take three deep breaths together to help us remember what we have enjoyed most about this ritual.'

6. CLOSING

It is good to make this formal, and for the family to develop its own regular way of making the closing, perhaps with a rhyme.

7. REINTEGRATION

Even if the meal has been part of the ritual, keep something special to mark the closing. This might be a fun treat that expresses the season; for example an equinox egg, or a summer solstice sun cake.

Community rituals

Ritual is an effective way to bring a community together and create a sense of shared purpose. From ancient times communities have shared their fears and hopes around the seasonal changes, celebrating the harvest, going into the darkness together, or welcoming in the spring. These are times when we can connect with each other through our differences.

1. PREPARATION

A small group of people needs to meet to plan the ritual. A location must be decided on. It can be inspiring to hold large rituals outside, but make sure you have a contingency plan in case of bad weather. When we hold ceremonies outside on the land, it is important to remember that the land may hold memories of other significant occasions, some of which may not be compatible with your ritual intention. Was it a scene of warfare, a cultivation ground, or a tapu place? By consulting with the local tribe, you may ascertain whether or not it is appropriate to use a particular site. For an outdoors location, the site may be marked by balloons, banners, or other means, if appropriate. For an indoors location, make sure the space is cleaned and made inviting. For people to experience a more expanded sense of themselves, they first need to feel they are entering sacred space. You may mark the threshold in some way, maybe with sticks or stones, so that people know when they are crossing over.

You can help people to come prepared on an inner level by asking them to bring a symbol or contemplate something in advance. When they arrive, a symbolic action at the threshold is helpful, such as touching the threshold, or cleansing with a bowl of water. They may be asked to observe silence when they enter the ritual space. There may be music playing, or drumming, to help them shift to an inner focus.

2. ORIENTATION

The leader(s) invoke the four directions: south (earth), west (water), north (fire) and east (air), placing or referring to symbols at each of these quarters. Invocations are made to the ancestors and the location as appropriate, and to the place of wholeness, or the meeting-place, that is marked by a symbol placed at the centre. People may also need to become oriented to each other, and one way of doing this is to ask them to say their names, going around the circle. This becomes a lot more powerful if people are willing to chant or call out their name, and have the whole group chant or call it back in exactly the same way. A statement of the purpose of the ritual makes people aware of the intention, or the season that is being celebrated.

3. CENTRING

If the group is seated or standing in a circle, centring may be done by inviting everyone to link hands, close their eyes and be aware of the ground beneath their feet. Singing a song together will also centre people.

4. ENACTMENT

Whatever happens here, it should involve everyone as participants, not just spectators, and at the same time, it should not take too long. An action that takes three minutes per person can stretch out to a two-hour ordeal with a group of 40: so people should be brief, and to the point. It is easiest if talking is not involved, or at the most a word or a short phrase. Sometimes the action can be performed simultaneously, such as when everyone is invited in their own time to take a stick symbolising some old belief or habit they wish to let go of, and to throw it into the fire, while somebody drumming raises energy.

5. DEEPENING

Silence allows deepening, and often with a large group, drumming or music helps hold the space for this to happen. Sometimes, in a very celebratory ritual, energies are heightened rather than deepened, with a release of energies taking place through dancing, shouting, waving of flags, tossing of balloons, or singing of songs. A procession may be another effective way of allowing the events of the ritual to be absorbed; or a spiral dance, where the procession moves in on itself in a spiral movement, and then out again.

6. CLOSING

The leader(s) formally close the ritual with a blessing, by offering thanks, or maybe a set phrase. In the Wiccan tradition these words are used:

> The circle is open
> But not broken
> May the peace of the Goddess go in our hearts
> Merry meet, and merry part

And merry meet again!
Blessed Be.

7. REINTEGRATION

This is the moment for feasting, talking, and a general release of energies. Some people may wish to take this process more slowly than others, and in some rituals space is designated for those who do not wish
to talk a lot, so that their wishes may be respected.

1. Gimbutas, p. xviii.

2. For a detailed outline of Celtic and
Maori cosmologies, see the final section
in this book.

3. Hiroa, pp. 480-500.

4. In the Northern Hemisphere, north
and south are reversed, with north
being the direction of earth, and
south of fire.

Seasonal rituals for Aotearoa

JUNE 21/22	*Winter solstice* *Te Maruaroa o te* *Takurua, Hotoke*	Song and dance; rebirth of the sun and Matariki; Christmas; Ra shifts towards Hine-raumati, guardian of land foods.
AUGUST 2	*First Light/Brigid* *Candlemas, Pakawera* *Hongonui*	Return of the Maiden, light and the flow of milk; initiation into womanhood. New beginnings.
SEPT 21/22	*Spring equinox* *Eostre, Te Koanga,* *Te Mahuru*	Rebirth, rise of the Green Man; the digging season; seeding the earth.
OCTOBER 31	*Flowering and* *Sap-rise, Beltane,* *Whiringanuku*	Spring Festival; National Green Day; maypole dancing. Trees and springs honoured.
DEC 21/22	*Summer solstice* *Te Maruaroa o te* *Raumati*	Celebration of the sun and the achievements of the year. Ra shifts towards Hine-takurua, guardian of sea food.
FEBRUARY 2	*First Fruits* *Lugnasad* *Lammas*	First loaves, grain, berries, the Lean Time: festival of the Half Harvest. Te Waru.
MARCH 21/22	*Autumn equinox* *Mabon, Poututerangi* *Te Ngahuru*	Harvest Festival: corn and kumara. Storing the goodness.
APRIL 30	*Last Light* *Samhain* *Halloween, Haratua*	Festival of the Dead; passing into the dark; Hine-nui-te-po; honouring the kuia and crone.

Winter Solstice

Te Maruaroa o te Takurua,

Te Hotoke

21 – 22 June

Winter solstice, the longest night of the year, is a time when nature seems to stand still; a key moment of deepening and withdrawing. Long shadows shape the land. Deciduous trees turn bare while native trees announce their greenness wherever mixed plantings occur. The sap has withdrawn, night closes in early and days are short.

In the bush, little seems to be happening, but puriri flowers appear to be more abundant now, attracting bellbirds, tuis and silvereyes. Kohekohe lets droop its long, white flower sprays and the sweet scent of whauwhaupaku (five-finger) wafts out from the winter-flowering clusters of tiny flowers.

Aotearoa

Matariki: Herald of the New Year

For the ancient Maori the new year began on the first new moon after the rising of Matariki (the Pleiades) in the eastern sky at dawn. The saying *Matariki kainga kore* (homeless Matariki)[3] refers to the constant travel of this constellation, which disappears from the sky to rest only once a year, on the waning moon of May. Matariki reappears in the tail of the Milky Way during the waning moon of June, which brings the start of the new year close to winter solstice.

Matariki is an important constellation associated with the providing of food, as expressed in the old saying *Nga kai a Matariki nana i ao ake ki runga* ('the foods of Matariki, by him/her brought forth').[4] The literal meaning of Matariki is 'little-eyes', referring to the appearance of this beautiful, jewel-like cluster of six or seven small stars.[5] The story of Matariki originates in the Southern Cook Islands (formerly known as the Hervey Islands), where it was said the god Tane became jealous of a certain very bright star that rivalled his own gift of stars to the heavens. He smashed the bright star into pieces and flung them across the sky. There they came to rest as 'little-eyes', fascinating people with their sparkling from that day on.[6]

Matariki may also be read as 'eyes of god', mata meaning 'eyes' and ariki 'god'. The stars were in fact seen as homes of the gods, a place where souls returned after death.[7]

The actual moment of first sighting could be an emotional occasion. Women would sing laments for the recent dead, or line up facing Matariki to greet the star cluster with a three-day festival of action songs and dances,[8] a custom that is being reclaimed by some Maori people today.[9] The important new year festival of celebration and feasting would then follow, the food being offered to Matariki with invocations:

> Matariki atua ka eke mai i te rangi e roa, e
> Whangainga iho ki te mata o te tau e roa, e.
> (Divine Matariki, come hither from the distant heavens,
> Bestow the first fruits of the year upon us.)[10]

The songs often referred to the sadness people felt when looking at Matariki, for this was where the dead went to after leaving the earth:

> Tirohia atu nei, ka wheturangitia Matariki,
> te whitu o te tau e whakamoe mai ra!
> He homai ana rongo kia komai atu au –
> ka mate nei au i te matapouri, i te mataporehu o roto i a au!
> (See where Matariki have risen over the horizon,
> the seven of the year winking up there!
> They come with their message that I may rejoice.
> Here I am full of sorrow, full of sadness within!)[11]

In another song Mere Reweti Taingunguru, Te Whanau-a-Apanui, refers to Matariki when lamenting the death of her husband, who was killed after leaving her at daybreak:

> Tera matariki huihui ana mai.

Ka ngaro ra, e, te whetu kukume ata.
(Behold the Pleiades are clustered above.
Lost, alas, is the star that hauls forth the dawn.)[12]

At the funeral rites of the tangihanga the 'seven of Matariki' are often mentioned by male orators in speeches that refer to the dead and the past. The female kaikaranga (callers) chant in ringing tones phrases like this:

Haere atu ra e kui	(Farewell old woman
Ki te paepae o Matariki	Go to the threshold of
O Rehua	the Pleiades...of Rehua
Haere atu ra	Farewell.)

When Matariki rose it was said *Tirohia atu nei ka wheturangitia Matariki, te whetu o te tau* ('Behold Matariki the star of the year has made its appearance').

The Pleiades have widespread significance throughout the world, the 'Pleiades year' beginning in late autumn or early winter being a feature of countries in South-east Asia, ancient Egypt, Sumeria, and Celtic Britain. The 'Pleiades year' is thought to have originated in southern India as one of the earliest systems of calculating the time of the new year in the lunar month of April/May or May/June, when, as with the Maori, it was marked by a First Fruits festival.[13]

This was not always the case for the Maori. Back in their Polynesian homeland the new year began about the time of summer solstice, when Matariki appeared on the horizon just after sunset. After arriving in Aotearoa the Maori shifted new year to the winter position celebrated today. Why did they do this? Perhaps the shift was a response to the change in agricultural practices, for while crops could be grown all year round in the islands, in the cooler new land the kumara, taro and gourd were restricted to a distinct seasonal cycle. Kumara was the most viable crop. Spring planting culminated in an autumn harvest, followed by storage of the tubers over the winter months. The two months after harvest were a relatively inert time in the agricultural cycle, and with the storehouses full it may have made

sense to feast and rejoice at the appearance of the star cluster that signalled the turning of the season, as so many cultures do after harvest.

Takurua, bringer of cold

Takurua was the name for both the star Sirius, the bringer of frost and
snow, and for winter itself, more commonly known today as Makariri
or Te Hotoke.[14] *Te anu o takurua* or *te anu o taku* refers to the cold of
this star.[15] If Takurua shone brightly it was said to be a sign of severe
frost to come.

Puanga: signal for the new year

The constellation of Orion was important to the Maori, for it contains
the star Puanga (Rigel), one of the intrinsically brightest stars known.
In winter Puanga is clearly visible. Its beauty was much admired, and
like Matariki it signalled the beginning of the new year, which occurred
on the first new moon after the rising of Puanga, between May and
June. In the Northern Hemisphere Orion appears as a giant with a star-
studded belt and bright sword. In the Southern Hemisphere Orion
faces up the other way and to the Maori appeared as a bird snare, with
shaft, perch and pewa, the blossom that was used to attract unsus-
pecting birds. The star Puanga was that blossom.[16] Its importance as a
winter star is referred to in the proverb *Te maruaroa, ko Puanga ka
kitea* ('during the solstice Rigel is seen').[17]

 The Chatham Islands Maori called it Puaka and referred to the
three bright stars (Orion's belt) as the whata or food store.[18] In other
parts the aphorism *Puanga kai rau* (Rigel of abundant food), associated Puanga with the early winter season of plenty.[19] Puanga was the
main star of the Ngai Tahu of Canterbury. The women watched it
closely to foretell the weather. If Puanga rose on the south side, it was
a sign of bad weather, but if it rose on the north, it was a good tohu
(omen). It was said to rise about June 6.[20] In the South Island the whare
purakau, the tapu school of learning, was opened each year at the
beginning of winter, with the rising of Puaka (Puanga) as the sign.[21]
In the North Island the Ngapuhi tribe greeted Puanga by sweeping

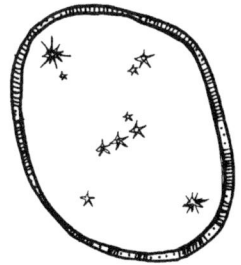

the marae ground, chanting invocations and making offerings of tapu food.

Pipiri, the first month

The first lunar month of the new year, spanning June/July, was referred to as te tahi o pipiri ('the first of pipiri'), pipiri meaning to cling together, i.e. out of the cold. Pipiri is also a star, or rather two stars that are close together and appear a little while before the Pleiades.[33] Pipiri is referred to in the saying *te po tutanga nui o pipiri* ('the division of the long night of pipiri'), which refers to the length of the winter nights. A 19th-century informant described this as the month when *Rua pipiri te kiri o nga mea katoa, rakau, tangata, ngarara, otaota* ('the skin of all things now contracts, of trees, people, insects, plants').[34] Tutakangahau, an elder of Maungapohatu (Tuhoe tribe) said it was when *kua piri nga mea katoa i te whenua i te matao, me te tangata* ('all things on earth contract because of the cold, including people').[35]

Ra the sun god

Winter solstice, known as hikumutu or te maruaroa o te hotoke, the time of the takanga o te ra ('changing of the sun'), marked another important shift. Ra was said to have two wives, both daughters of Tangaroa. He spent half the year with Hine-takurua, the Winter Woman in the south, far out on the ocean, for she was identified with the work of fishing. At the maruaroa of winter, he was said to begin his return to his other wife, Hine-raumati, the Summer Woman who dwells on land and was associated with the gathering of forest food, game and the growing of crops. Old men would observe at winter solstice, 'The sun is returning to land to dwell with the Summer Maid.'[22]

Bush foods

The bush offered little edible fruit at this season: kawakawa perhaps, or papauma (broadleaf) berries that were eaten when other fruits were scarce; kareao (supplejack), miro, or ureure, the fruit of the kiekie which was now ripe and was eaten fresh.[23]

The bird-preserving season

Although forest berries palatable to humans were ending their season, there was abundant food for birds. Hine-raumati was in charge of the preserving of birds, and she now came into her own, for the dawn rising of Matariki was the sign for the preserving season to begin. As the proverb states, *Ka kitea a Matariki, na kua maoka te hinu* ('when the Pleiades are seen, then the preserved flesh is cooked').[24] Food that was preserved by the huahua method, i.e. in its own fat, was regarded as one of the special delicacies of Hine-raumati, especially tui and kereru (wood pigeon, also known as kukupa) which preserved better than kaka, the other main bird caught in winter.[25] The bird-snaring season was now in full swing.

The kaka was moulting and grew fat, seeking food on the ground, which made it easy to catch. Berry-feeding tui came into their plump season from May to August and were known as koko.[26] They became so sluggish that they could be taken by hand, especially on cold nights. First the men marked the roosting trees with rangiora or silver fern leaves, placed white side up. Then at midnight they would light torches and return to the bush where the birds huddled for shelter on the lower branches and could easily be lifted off. The passivity of such fat tui was used as a warning to sleepy warriors in the proverb *He koko whakamoe, ka mate te tangata* ('when sleeping like a tui, a person will die'). The kereru (wood pigeon) also grew fat, feeding on tawa and other berries, and was called whaturua[27] at this time. It was particularly susceptible to being caught in large numbers after eating miro berries, for the berries induced extreme thirst. Snarers took advantage of this by setting up water troughs, then chanting karakia (invocations) to charm the birds to drink so they could be snared.

Huge numbers of birds were taken in this period. According to one account, 4500–5000 kereru, kaka and tui were taken in one month from a Hokianga forest valley during the miro fruiting.[28] In the folktale *Ko Pukoroauahi* ('The Boy and the Pigeons'), the boy catches 170 baskets of kereru at one stream. Once cooked and preserved, they fill 70 calabashes.[29]

Within living memory, we have the recollections of Tamati

Kurupae of Taupo:

> ...in the winter, the takurua, we went to Tauhara Mountain bird-hunting. That was our great bird-mountain; that was our parent that supplied us with our stores of manu-huahua. The bush was full of birds, especially the kereru (pigeon) and koko (tui, parson bird). We caught them in snares arranged above wai-tuhi, small troughs shaped like canoes, which we filled with water; these were set in the driest parts of the bush, so that the birds might be tempted to fly down there and drink. We speared them, too, with long barbed wooden spears. The kaka parrot was plentiful; we caught it with mutu kaka, elbowed wooden snares, rigged with running flax-string tackle, which we set up in the rata trees. With these contrivances, camping there for many days, we caught great numbers of birds, which we cooked and preserved in their own fat in airtight vessels of totara bark. And the birds never decreased in those days when snares and spear were used more than the gun. There are birds there still, and it is pleasing to hear the koko, that manu rangatira, but the old days of abundance of food have gone – aue![30]

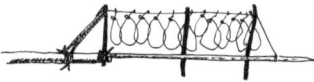

Proverbs referred to the bounty, comparing it with bounty from that other food basket, the kaimoana (sea food): *He tutu kaka ki uta, he toka koura ki te moana* ('a kaka-snaring tree on land, a crayfish rock at sea'), and the Waiapu proverb *He kaka tawari ki Hikurangi, ke moki ki te moana* ('a kaka feeding on tawari berries of Hikurangi is as fat as the moki fish of the ocean').[31] A Tuhoe proverb compared the kaka's strong beak, that would tear snares set for other birds, with the barracouta's rending of nets at sea: *He kaka kei uta, he manga kei te moana.*

Women sometimes took part in snaring, being allocated their own trees. They were most active however in the work of cooking and preserving. When the catch had been processed and the manu-huahua (fat-preserved bird flesh) stored in gourds (or kelp bags in the South Island where gourds did not grow), the Ngati Porou people returned home from their forest camps, making a spectacular entrance. Karakia were chanted as they went, and on reaching the village the tapu chant *Tau o Uenuku* rang forth. The forest party was received in complete silence, then after another karakia the gourds were dropped to the ground. The way they fell was taken as an omen for each bird-snarer, and only after they had fallen and the last karakia had been uttered could silence be broken by the welcomers, who now broke into an enthusiastic powhiri (action song of welcome).[32]

Birds preserved by the huahua method made a highly prized food and the gourds they were stored in became important centre-pieces at feasts. They were fitted with wooden carved legs and necks and decorated with bird feathers that matched the species contained inside.

Fish

Women now went to the pataka (food houses) to bring out fish that had been sun-dried in summer for winter eating. The appearance of Matariki was a sign for the catching of the korokoro (lamprey eel) to begin.[36] Maori fishers caught huge quantities of eels during the migrations by making diversionary channels or weirs, setting eel pots or catching them with a moenu (bob) made of split flax and wiwi (rushes) baited with worms.[37]

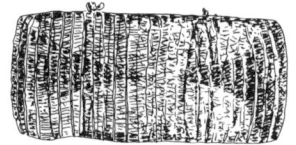

Firewood

An additional activity in winter was the collection of firewood so that people could keep warm. As the proverb says, *Te wahie ka waia mo takurua, te kai ka mahia mo tau* ('firewood is sought in winter, food all year round').[38]

Weather predictions

Winter was characterised by its wetness as well as its coldness. As the proverb says: *Matariki tapuapua*: ('when pools lie everywhere')[39]. The heavy rains of early winter were also linked to the star Aotahi (Canopus) and referred to as kohi o Aotahi. They were regarded as a sign for the first migration of inanga (whitebait) to go to the sea and give birth to their young.[40]

Aotahi was a very tapu star, appearing at the start of the winter solstice season: 'Ko Aotahi te upoko o nga whetu; hei te Maruaroa te kite ai i te ata' ('Canopus is the principal star; it is seen in the morning during the solstice').[41] It was carefully watched as a forecaster of the winter weather; as one authority said, 'If its rays extend towards the south it foretells rain and snow, an inclement season; if toward the north, a mild season follows.'[42] The proverb Haere i mua i te aroaro o Atutahi ('when you go, travel ahead of Atutahi/Aotahi') advises travellers to journey before the onset of winter.[43]

The migrating cuckoos had now long gone, and their absence after harvest paralleled the fallow time in the agricultural season. Various stories told of cuckoos going to the beds of lakes and staying buried there under the mud during winter, or of them burying themselves in the earth and turning into lizards.[44] Such stories bear a resemblance to European tales of the Maiden's journey to the underworld and re-appearance in spring. But for the Maori, winter was not just a journey of withdrawal as the earth closed down her growing season; it was also a season for hunting and gathering, and the season for war. With young men freed from attending to crops, they could consider the injunction of the winter proverb, 'You need something to go with the kumara', and go on raiding parties or to avenge wrongs. Tumatauenga, the god of war, was the god of this season.[45]

Pagan Europe

The birth of the sun

In the old neolithic societies of Europe, winter solstice was a significant time. The wise ones went to a great deal of care to ascertain the exact moment of solstice, often using stone circles to help them to mark both the turning of the sun and the position of the moon at that point. It is thought that people took part in ring dances on the sites of the stone circles, as well as rituals to encourage the awakening of the sun and the life-force within themselves.[48]

Winter solstice continued to be an important festival in the agricultural societies of Europe. For the six preceding months darkness had

increased, stealing light from the margins of the day. It seemed as if life itself was being swallowed up. After the bounty of harvest, all nature had begun to die, with leaves shrivelling on the trees and dropping to reveal stark, bare branches. The colour green faded from the earth. Death, it seemed, was making an irrevocable advance.

Then a significant event occurred: the sun turned. Light was reborn to the world, and after a few days the change was discernible to all. The rebirth of the sun marked the vital moment of renewed hope, when continuity of life for crops, animals and people was assured. People could rejoice, feast and celebrate, just as they had done in neolithic societies and the civilisations of the Middle East.

There, winter solstice was symbolised by the birth of a divine male child from the dark womb of the Goddess. There was no father, as the Goddess herself was all-sufficient. Priests announced the event in dramatic rituals: in Syria they emerged from underground cave shrines at midnight, announcing, 'The Virgin Goddess has brought forth! The light increases!'[49] In Egypt they held up the image of an infant for all the worshippers to see, and cried out, 'Here is the sun child of the Heavenly Goddess! Let us celebrate his birth!' In Persia they celebrated the goddess Aargatis's birthing of the sun god Mithra, who was known as the Unconquered Sun and whose birthday fell on 25 December, the time when the increased light was perceptible. In Babylon it was Astarte, Queen of Heaven, who gave birth to the divine child. In Alexandria people flocked to the temple of Kore to rejoice at the winter solstice miraculous birth. The child of light had many names: Horus, Osiris, Helios, Dionysus or Aeon.[50]

The sonne of all the world
is dimme and darke

The earth now lacks her
wonted light
And all we dwell in deadly night
O heavie herse.
(Edmund Spenser,
The Shepheardes Calender).[46]

...the world's whole sap is sunk
(John Donne, 'A Nocturnal
Upon S Lucies Day Being the
Shortest Day')[47]

Rome

These ancient traditions were reflected in the solstice festivals of Rome. December was a quieter month in terms of work, with most of the ploughing and sowing over, leaving time at last to relax. From 17 to 23 December Romans celebrated the birthday of the Unconquered One in the Feast of the Unconquered Sun, known as the Saturnalia, or *Dies Natalis Solis Invicti*. Saturn was the god of agriculture and the golden age, but also of time and death. It was a time of high festivity, the

Saturnalia being the most popular Roman festival, when 'all Rome went mad'.[51]

Celtic and Anglo-Saxon Britain

In Celtic mythology the goddess Rhiannon gave birth to Pryderio at the darkest time and it was also the birth of the child of light, known as Mabon. In the old Celtic Coligny calendar,[52] the lunar month spanning November/December was the time of the 'darkest depths' and that of December/January was known as 'the cold time'. While the Celtic year ended and was reborn at Samhain, this was later taken over by the Anglo-Saxon year which ended and began again at Yule in December. For the Anglo-Saxons winter solstice represented the triumph of one force over another, for now the Oak King, god of the waxing year, conquered the Holly King, god of the waning year. The two gods were twins, one light and one dark, who were caught in an eternal rivalry. Their battle came to be played out in the mumming plays of winter solstice where the death of one character (reminiscent of the 'light twin') symbolises the killing of the crops by the chill of winter, and his revival by 'the doctor' symbolises the coming of spring. In one version the light twin becomes St. George who, after being revived by the doctor, kills the dark Turkish Knight, then cries out that alas, he has slain his brother:

> Only behold and see what I have been and done,
> Cut and slain my brother just like the evening sun.[53]

Fire symbolism

In the winter solstice rituals of Europe, greenery and fire are two key elements, for these were what people most wanted to magic back into their lives. Candles were lit to invoke fire, but the most important focus of fire symbolism was the yule-log, which the Druids, the Celtic priests of ancient Britain, lit in honour of the god Thor. Thor stood for warmth, light, and the continuance of life. Yule, the Festival of Rebirth, lasted 12 days (now known as 'the twelve days of Christmas'), a number which coincides with the number of days left over in the lunar year. The name Yule comes from old Saxon and Norse words meaning 'light' or 'sun', and also has origins in Old Norse *Iul*, meaning wheel.[54] This was the moment of the turning of the wheel of the year.

The lighting of the yule-log was a custom that continued among the Scandinavians, Slavs and Celts in post-Christian times. Families brought in the log, ideally an ash[55] or oak, on Christmas Eve, and decorated it with bright ribbons and greenery, usually ivy. In Britain people came to believe that the yule log should burn for 12 hours without going out, a condensation of the 12 days of burning in older times.[56] If it went out, there would be bad luck for a year. The new yule-log was lit from a fragment of the old as a sign of continuity. In many places the ashes were sprinkled in gardens, fields and orchards for fertility and to invoke the regenerative power of fire. Robert Herrick's poem captures well the spirit of the yule-log:

> Come, bring with a noise,
> My merrie, merrie boyes
> The Christmas Log to the firing;
> While my good Dame, she
> Bids ye all be free;
> And drink to your hearts desiring.
>
> With the last yeeres brand
> Light the new block...[57]

Green symbolism

Greenery in winter solstice rituals was brought in to celebrate the triumph of the life-force. In Egypt a 12-leafed palm was used to symbolise the completion of the year.[58] In Rome people decorated the temples with evergreens, especially holly, and exchanged holly twigs to wish each other good health and well-being. They also decorated pine or fir trees at winter solstice, with streamers, a bird, bells, and ornaments of gold and silver. The pine tree was the sacred tree of the vegetation god Attis, and the fir belonged to the Teutonic god Odin, known in Britain

as Woden.[59]

In Britain, holly, ivy and mistletoe stood out as rare splashes of green among the bare branches of the forest. Communities gathered the plants and brought them inside for decoration, not only because the plants were evergreen but also because they bore fruit in winter.

Mistletoe

To the Druids, mistletoe was especially significant. The way it grew high in treetops without any apparent root or trunk connection to the earth made it appear magical. It was valued most highly when found growing on the oak, the Druids' most sacred tree. Moreover, its white berries turned golden after picking; hence its name 'the golden bough'.[60] Druids regarded the poisonous white berries as drops of semen of the oak god.[61] Originally, human sacrifices were made before mistletoe cutting; later it was white oxen that were taken. On the sixth day of the moon the mistletoe was cut from the oak groves with a golden sickle, caught in a white cloth so as not to touch the ground and lose its magical power, and given to the people to hang over their doorways. There it served as protection against death by arrows, and also against fire and lightning.[62] It was said to have healing powers, a widespread belief that has continued through to modern times (it is held by the Ainu of Japan). In modern Irish and Scottish Gaelic, the word for mistletoe is *uil-ioc*, meaning 'all-healer'.[63]

Ivy and holly

Ivy and holly (sacred to Saturn) symbolised eternal life, being evergreen, and were thought to bring good luck. The red holly berries were seen as drops of blood of the Teutonic goddess Hel (Holle). She was the goddess of spinning, weaving, and flax cultivation, whose festival was honoured in Scandinavia during the 12 days around winter solstice; during this time no one would spin flax. Winter solstice still marks the new year in Scandinavia today.[64] Later, boughs of the evergreens were bound in wreath-like forms known as kissing boughs and hung from the ceiling, a custom that has survived in the practice of kissing under the mistletoe. Men sang songs to their symbolic plant, the holly:

> Then Heigh ho the holly
> This Life is most jolly[65]

and women to their sacred plant, the ivy, which was regarded as feminine.[66] As the Elizabethan song line went:

> Ivy is soft and meek of speech.[67]

Shakespeare refers to it as

> The female ivy[that]
> So enrings the barky finders of the elm.[68]

Rivalry between the two plants was expressed in various songs, such as the 15th-century refrain:

> Holver[holly] and Heivy [ivy] made a grete party
> Who should have the maistry
> In londès where they go...[69]

Carols

People sang and danced carols, which were originally not just songs but singing circle dances. The dancing season in Europe went from autumn through till the end of winter, an echo perhaps of the practice of tribal people throughout the world, who place a taboo on dancing before the harvest is safely in.[70] Some of the carols still sung today go back to pagan times, such as, 'The Holly and the Ivy':

> The holly and the ivy
> Now both are full well grown
> Of all the trees that are in the wood,
> The holly bears the crown

with its refrain which harks back to the pagan horned god and the male custom of donning deer antlers as part of ancient rituals.

> Oh, the rising of the sun
> And the running of the deer.[71]

Wassailing

The celebratory practice of wassailing – going from house to house with songs of good cheer – grew out of an early pagan ritual where groups of morris dancers danced to encourage a good apple harvest in the year to come.[72]

Medieval celebrations

Through medieval times the rituals continued. A master of ceremonies known as the Lord of Misrule was appointed to look after the festivities. He was usually the fool or jester, whose job it was to keep things merry, arrange practical jokes and encourage burlesque and buffoonery. It was a time when people could let their hair down, but also on a deeper level acknowledge the importance of the greening forces of nature. The feast could not begin without the symbolic entry of greenness and so a participant called the Surveyor shouted out 'Wassail!', a word coming from Saxon *Wass Hael* meaning 'to your health'. The guests sat silent. He then asked the most honoured guest for permission for the feast to begin. 'No,' came the reply, 'not until the First Foot crosses the threshold.' Then the sound of bells would be heard, and a dark-haired man dressed in green bounded in from the back of the hall. His ankles ringing, an evergreen branch in one hand, he leaped over a line of green vegetation, took off his cap, and handed it round for the guests to toss coins into. Now the mead could be drunk and the feasting proceed.[73]

This was the Green Knight, also known as the Wild Man, Holly King or Holly Knight. He was the embodiment of the spirit of nature and a reminder of the greening force that surged in both vegetation and humans.

Christian Europe: Christmas

How was the festival of Christmas born, and what connection does it have with winter solstice? The Gospels said nothing about the date of the birth of Christ and it wasn't celebrated in the early Church. However, the Christians of Egypt eventually came to believe he was born on 6 January, a belief that spread throughout the East until by the fourth century it was widely accepted. In the West a different date was adopted, due to a conscious decision made by Augustine and other Roman church leaders. They fixed the date of Christmas at 25 December, seeing the advantage of planting the Christian festival into the already fertile soil of the pagan winter solstice rituals.[74] After all, the birth of the divine Sun Child was already a feature of the mythology and it was but a small step to see Christ as the 'Sun of Righteousness'.[75] As one Christian Syrian writer recorded:

> The reason why the fathers transferred the celebration of the sixth of January to the twenty-fifth of December was this. It was a custom of the heathen to celebrate on the same twenty-fifth of December the birthday of the Sun, at which they kindled lights in token of festivity. In these solemnities and festivities the Christians also took part. Accordingly when the doctors of the Church perceived that the Christians had a leaning to this festival, they took counsel and resolved that the true Nativity should be solemnised on that day and the festival of the Epiphany on the sixth of January.[76]

The timing also suited the rhythm of the year, the time of pause in the cycle of intense work on the land. Gradually a transfer of devotional allegiance took place. In early Christian Rome, where people decorated churches and houses with holly at Yule, the holly now came to signify Christmas, its prickles symbolising Christ's crown of thorns and its red berries his blood.[77] The berries of the 'male' holly were said to protect against witches, a belief that distorted the ancient meaning of the berries as signifying the blood of the Goddess. Her own symbol was turned against her and she became the witch, a figure to be feared.

Puritan disapproval of Christmas

Throughout medieval times people celebrated Christmas with high-spirited revelry, clowning, buffoonery and much feasting. The Puritans did not approve of all the practices: bringing evergreens into the house was forbidden, right through to the 1640s when a theologian wrote of the customs in Europe: 'Among other trifles which are set up during Christmas time instead of God's Word, is the Christmas tree, or fir tree which is put up in the home and decorated with dolls and sugar!'[78] In England, during the reign of Elizabeth I, Puritans did their best to stop the pagan fun instigated by the Lord of Misrule, because of the way it mocked the Church (along with everything and everyone in high places). Such was their reformist zeal and dislike of revelry that in 1652 they abolished Christmas itself by Act of Parliament, with a proclamation stating:

> No observation shall be had of the five-and-twentieth day of December, commonly called Christmas Day; nor any solemnity used or exercised in churches upon that day in respect thereof.[79]

A Puritan pamphlet of the time makes it quite clear how Roman Catholicism and pagan ways were linked in the Puritan mind:

> Christmas Day, the old Heathens' Feasting Day in honour to Saturn their Idol-God, the Papists' Massing Day, taking to hearth the Heathenish customs, Popish superstitions, ranting fashions, fearful provocations, horrible abominations committed against the Lord, and his Christ on that day and dayes following…[80]

For the next eight years no Christmas masses or public festivals were held, but in 1660 the monarchy was restored and the old revelries were reinstated.

Victorian Christmas

In the United Kingdom it wasn't until the Victorian era that the Christmas festival as we know it came into form. In many ways it was a Victorian invention, aided by Charles Dickens and Prince Albert, the husband of Queen Victoria, upholders of a sentimental view of family life. Prince Albert is said to have introduced the Christmas tree in 1840 from his native Germany.[81] There it dated back to the old pagan Yule celebrations, along with the boar's head stuffed with apples, the lighting of candles and exchanging of gifts.[82]

The Christmas card

The Victorian Age being a materialistic one, card manufacturers seized the opportunity to make a commercial success of Christmas, borrowing and promoting the character of Old Father Christmas from the mummer's plays – not a main character, but one who seemed to suit the occasion. The first cards show him arriving in a hot air balloon, an image which did not catch the public imagination, despite the contemporary nature of this means of travel. The following year a rival firm tried a sleigh drawn by reindeer, an inspired gesture that drew on more ancient mythology.[83] The public loved it. Whether they knew it or not, the imagery resonated with the German/Scandinavian Woden/Oden, the vegetation god who gave out presents from his sky chariot, which was drawn by the eight-toed horse Sleipnir. Being a sky god, his feet never touched the ground and hence his ability to enter houses via chimneys.

Santa Claus

As German/Teutonic symbolism cross-fertilised in Britain, so did Dutch symbolism in the United States in the form of San Nicolaas, brought by the Dutch settlers and later corrupted into Santa Claus. A lover of children, he gave out presents on 6 December, a date that was later transferred to 25 December.

Thus we have the modern Christmas, a festival liberally strewn with pagan symbolism of sun-birth and greening, now well integrated with one curious exception: the English Church has continued to reject mistletoe as part of the Christmas decorations, due to its pagan origin.[84]

Rituals for today

How can we best celebrate winter solstice today, with ritual that connects us to the levels of meaning of this moment in the seasonal cycle?

Maori people who are reclaiming the old rituals around the greeting of Matariki and the start of the new cycle are already answering this question. Many tribal groups have officially adopted the Maori calendar, and use the old terms in speech and correspondence.

Pakeha communities drawing on the traditions of old Europe are celebrating the birth of the sun at winter solstice in many different ways. For years people have drummed up the sun through the night in the crater of an Auckland volcano. My women's ritual group holds a cave ritual where participants let go of the old year, welcoming in the new cycle. Using sites which may have other significance to the tangata whenua raises questions of respect for the energies already constelled around a particular place, and the need to communicate with the kaumatua (elders) in order to gain their sanction. With the cave ritual, this communication has taken place and permission has been granted.

Most people miss out on the significance of winter solstice, for although Christmas with all its solstice links is still celebrated, it takes place at entirely the wrong time of year. Here in the Southern Hemisphere it becomes a summer festival, but is acted out as if it were still winter. Thus we have the anomalies of 'snow' being sprayed out of cans on to shop windows and pine trees, and the exchange of cards figuring robins, holly and other Northern Hemisphere winter Yule symbols.

If we were to shift Christmas to its true location at the darkest night and the onset of winter we would make a rich connection with the old festivals of the European heritage. This is when it makes sense to feast and be with people, to light fires and enjoy warm cooked food, for we are celebrating the rebirth of the sun. It is natural to want to enjoy good company at this season and to gather together with our loved ones, as people have done from ancient times. For Christians, to celebrate the birth of Christ, the 'light of the world', at this time, would be to link the spiritual event with the rhythms of the earth, just as it was by the early Church leaders.

Many people are indeed already making this shift, and enjoying a mid-winter Christmas. To do so is consistent with Maori tradition also, where the appearance of Matariki, the food provider, who signals the beginning of a new year and the preserving of food, likewise brings reason to celebrate and to feast.

In both traditions song and dance form part of the solstice feast: the action songs of the Maori women as they greet Matariki, and the carols, the old singing circle dances of the European tradition. We celebrate the completion of a cycle and give thanks, drawing on the company of friends and families in order to support us as we face the cold months ahead. I have tried without success to discover the dance form of an old carol; however, some of the songs have been preserved. They have a bouncing, happy rhythm and may be used as circle dances if people wish to experiment and find their own forms. The very simplest would be:

- Link hands in a circle. Everyone moves in the direction of the sun (ie. anti-clockwise for the Southern Hemisphere) for four steps.

- Everyone moves clockwise for four steps.

- Everyone takes four steps into the centre, raising their linked arms as they do so. This action brings energy up to greet the sun.

- Everyone takes four steps back, lowering their arms.

Suitable carols would be 'I Saw Three Ships', 'The Twelve Days of Christmas' and 'Lord of the Dance'. Other carols that link back to old Europe are 'The Holly and the Ivy' and 'Green Grow'th the Holly'.[85]

Another suitable winter solstice dance would be the ancient Greek 'Dance to Apollo', with its actions invoking the rising of the sun.[86]

On a more inward level, winter solstice is an opportunity to reflect

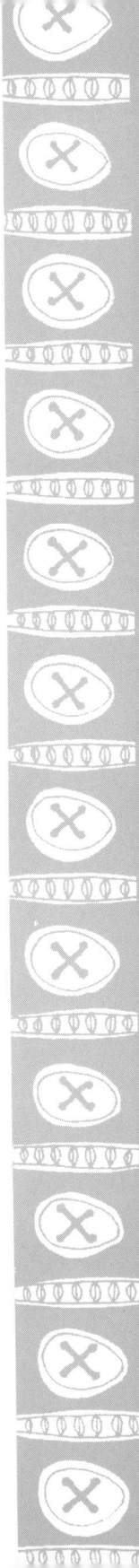

on what lies within our own darkness that is awaiting birth. What have we offered to the Great Mother for gestation and holding? As we light candles at solstice we might focus on what we are kindling within ourselves.

Preserved food might feature in our feasts, reflecting the fact that in both Maori and European traditions fresh supplies were scarce and it was time to draw on the food stores: dried fish in both cultures, salted or dried meats in Europe, with dried fruit and grains; kumara in Aotearoa. The European tradition of roasting a bird (goose, turkey or chicken) at Christmas is similar to the eating of huahua-preserved bird flesh in Maori culture, this being the game season. For drinks, mulled wine, cider mead and hot punch are traditional.

We may burn a log, lighting it from a fragment of the log of the previous year, as in the old Yule customs, signifying continuity of life. The blazing fire invites good company and gives warmth and good cheer. Perhaps we may find some flowering whauwhaupaku (five-finger), kohekohe or puriri and celebrate the continuous greening of this land throughout the year, or bring in a branch of pine to decorate, in memory of the old European tradition of tree worship. We can light candles on the tree or in the house to invoke the sun. The tree could be decorated with two kinds of symbols: sun symbols to celebrate the birth of the sun, and star symbols to celebrate the appearance of Matariki and Puanga. Children could be encouraged to make suns and stars, and to watch for the constellations of Orion and the Pleiades, maybe making drawings of them or featuring them on their solstice cards. They could also make images of native birds for the tree, especially the kaka, kereru and tui, whose plump flesh in winter used to provide such an important source of protein for the Maori. Miro berries could become important symbols as the true winter berries of this land, and a vital source of food for the native birds. The miro and kereru could end up replacing the holly and the robin.

By moving Christmas to 21/22 June we give ourselves a chance to enjoy it to the full. We also provide an opportunity to take notice of winter solstice; instead of it being a low point of the year it could become a warm and affirming time of celebration, when we draw strength to face the cold of winter.

1. Riley, 73-11.

2. Baxter, p. 3.

3. Riley, 73-10.

4. Best, *Agric*, p. 215.

5. See Best, *Astron*, p. 52 for his note on how Colenso was impressed at the keenness of Maori eyesight, remarking that they could see seven or more stars in the Pleiades cluster, whereas Europeans could see only six.

6. Frazer, *Corn & Wild*, p. 312.

7. Ruth Tai, pers. comm. The Pleiades were also important to the Aborigines of Australia, as the bringers of rain. The Aborigines would sing and dance to the Pleiades to get their blessings. The constellation was also associated with bringing heat since it rises higher and higher during summer, reaches the highest point during the summer's heat, then disappears in winter. See Frazer, *Corn & Wild*, pp. 307, 308, 318.

8. Orbell, *Poetry*, p. 100.

9. Matariki was joyfully welcomed in this way throughout the Pacific. The Abipones of Paraguay also greeted the Pleiades with joyful shouts and music (flute and horn) when he reappeared from his absence, which was regarded as his time of sickness. See Frazer, *Corn & Wild*, pp. 308-309.

10. Best, *Agric,* p. 107.

11. Orbell, *Poetry*, pp. 78-79, and *Nat World,* p. 71.

12. Ngata, *Nga Moteatea* II, pp. 44-45.

13. Best, *Time*, pp. 17 and 24, and *Astron*, p. 55.

14. Beattie, pp. 49-50. His informant Teone Taare Tikao of Ngai Tahu commented that south of Canterbury winter was called, not takurua but makariri (cold).

15. Brougham, 1963, p. 15.

16. Best, *Astron*, p. 48.

17. Best, *Time*, p. 48.

18. Best, *Astron*, p. 47.

19. Best, *Astron*, p.48, and Brougham, p. 52.

20. Beattie, p. 49 and Best, *Astron*, p.48.

21. Best, *Astron*, p. 49.

22. Best, *Astron*, p. 18 and *Time*, p. 49.

23. Makereti, p. 208.

24. Brougham, 1963, p. 43, and Best, *Time*, p 53.

25. Beattie, p. 136.

26. Best, *Forest*, p. 292. Koko means 'to thrust or scoop', and refers to the tui's way of getting rid of superfluous fat by thrusting its beak into its body, so that the fat oozes out.

27. Best, *Forest*, p. 233.

28. Best, *Forest*, p. 242.

29. Orbell, *Folktales*, pp. 59-63.

30. Pomare, p. 179.

31. Best, *Forest*, p. 193.

32. Best, *Forest*, pp. 286-289.

33. Best, *Astron*, p. 59.

34. Best, *Time*, p. 22.

35. Best, *Time*, p. 19.

36. Best, *Astron*, p. 53.

37. Beattie, p. 138.

38. Brougham, p. 121.

39. Best, *Astron*, p. 53.

40. Best, *Astron*, p. 43.

41. Best, *Time*, p.48.

42. Best, *Astron*, p. 42.

43. Brougham, p. 117 and Riley, 73-8.

44. Best, *Forest*, p. 337.

45. Simmons, p. 16.

46. Sitwell, Vol 1, p. 137.

47. Hayward, ed, p. 80.

48. Gimbutas, p. 313.

49. Neumann, p. 312. He points out that originally the birth of the light of the new moon was greeted in this way, but later this changed into celebrating the birth of the sun child: see p. 314.

50. Frazer, *Bough*, p. 472.

51. Harrowven, p. 133.

52. The bronze engraved Coligny calendar was named after the place in Northern France where it was discovered. Thought to be the work of the Druids, it gives detailed information on the Celtic lunar and solar cycles.

53. Rowan, p. 107.

54. Durdin-Robertson, p. 201.

55. Whistler, p. 58.

56. Kightly, p. 238.

57. Quoted in F. Muir, p. 58.

58. Durdin-Robertson, p. 201.

59. Cooper, p. 52, and Harrowven, p. 154.

60. Rutherford, p. 65.

61. Walker, *Dict.*, p. 447.

62. Harrowven, p. 152.

63. Ross, *Celts*, p. 141.

64. *Lesbian Lore*, p. 11.

65. Barker, p. 115; from Shakespeare, *As You Like It*, 11, vii.

66. It was also associated with Dionysus: see Whistler, p. 41.

67. Barker, p. 115, from Chambers & Sigwick, *Lyrics*, no. cxxxviii.

68. Barker, p. 130; from Shakespeare, *A Midsummer Night's Dream*, IV, i, 46-7.

69. F. Muir, p. 62.

70. Sachs, p. 68.

71. Cooper, p. 45.

72. Campanelli, p. 209.

73. Cosman, p. 93.

74. Frazer, *Bough*, p. 472.

75. It is interesting that Tennyson in *Idylls of the King* locates King Arthur's birth at Yule. King Arthur was a 'saviour' who spanned the transition between pagan and Christian practices.

76. Frazer, *Bough*, p. 472.

77. Kightly, p. 73.

78. Campanelli, p. 212.

79. F. Muir, p. 92.

80. F. Muir, p. 91.

81. There is in fact evidence that it had appeared a little earlier than this. See Whistler, pp. 29-30.

82. Kightly, p. 73.

83. Harrowven, p. 158.

84. Kightly, p. 74, writing in 1980. York Minster, where mistletoe is placed on the altar at Christmas, is the exception.

85. For music and words of all these, see Langstaff's excellent *The Christmas Revels Songbook*.

86. Tape and dance instructions available from Renaissance International, 2147 Oakland Drive, Kalamazoo, MI 49008-2269, USA. Phone (616)385-2592; fax (616)385-2441.

First Light

Imbolc, Oimelc, Brigid,
Candlemas, Pakawera, Hongonui

2 August

The moment of First Light lies exactly midway between winter solstice and spring equinox. It is a time of stirrings, when the increasing light is felt but not quite believed in. The weather is full of changes, from brilliant sunbursts to sharp, sudden showers, which bring an abrupt chill to the atmosphere. The unwary are caught without coats. At one moment the promise of spring hovers in the air; the next, winter leaps out and catches us by the throat. It is a changeable time, yet a time of promise.

It is a quiescent time in the bush, as if the new light has not yet penetrated there. On the bush floor, green-hooded orchids are flowering and mushrooms pop out of the damp into the gentle new warmth, but trees are still gathering their buds. Kumarahou, tawari, puawananga (clematis), karaka and kowhai are preparing to flower, but have not yet burst forth. This season precedes the drama of spring; it is a time of gathering, of preparation.

The quiet of the bush stands in contrast to the new energy of the open garden, where exotic plants respond to the warming of the earth. Bulbs push their spears through sun-fingered soil to flaunt delicate colours and sweet perfumes. Narcissi and daffodils abound, while primroses sit delicately upon their nests of leaves. Daphne lets loose the last of its pink fragrance. Snowdrops cluster in shady corners; polyanthus flashes with bright colour, and pink clouds of flowering cherry waft among bare branches, contrasting with the frothy, white clusters of plum blossom.

Aotearoa

For Maori, First Light comes in the second lunar month of the year, Pakawera (July/August), described as ruarua huangohingohi ('few and withered')[3], when *ka haere memenge nga rau o nga mea katoa i te huka* ('the leaves of all things become shrivelled by frost')[4] To the Tuhoe it was Hongonui, when *kua tino matao te tangata, me te tahutahu ahi, ka painaina* ('people are now extremely cold and kindle fire to warm themselves')[5] Kereru (wood pigeons) run short of berries. They are forced to turn to unpalatable kowhai leaves and consequently lose condition, the leaves giving their flesh an unpleasant smell which made them unsuitable for eating.[6] The bird and rat-gathering seasons were now ending and people came home from the forest.

Fish

However, the young eels begin to swim upstream and could now be caught, and at sea the moki were said to be growing fat. The inanga (whitebait), went up the rivers 'like a company of soldiers in great numbers, keeping a column two or three feet wide', and were caught in large numbers in oval hoop-nets known as haokoeaea. They were caught in July, August and early September and were always eaten fresh.[7]

The kotukutuku tree is bare, being the one native tree to lose its leaves. This event figures in a proverb used to chide those who absented themselves at this time, for if conditions were suitable, the ground needed to be prepared for the planting season: *I whea koe i te ngahorotanga o te rau o te kotukutuku?* – where were you when the fuchsia leaves fell?[8] Workers were kept busy heaping up the earth into mounds that would receive the spring kumara seed shoots. Matariki, the Pleiades constellation, watched over them, and this is referred to in the proverb *Matariki ahunga nui* ('the Pleiades with many mounds heaped up').[9]

Planets and stars

Visible now in the morning sky is Kopu, the name for the planet Venus when it appeared as a 'morning star' in the cool season. She was said to be a companion of the sun and to give warning of the dawn. Kopu was associated with female beauty, just as Venus is in the European tradition, for this planet is exceptionally brilliant. Astronomers say that the special radiance of Venus is due to the fact that it is shrouded in dense cloud cover, which reflects light more readily than any other substance.[10] Maori people said an attractive woman was *mehemea ko Kopu e rere ana i te pae* ('like the star Venus as it rises above the horizon').[11]

Whakaahu (Castor of Castor and Pollux), a star associated with summer, rises now.[12] Kaiwaka, which gave its name to the third lunar month of August/September may also be coming into view.[13]

Parearau (Jupiter) rises in the morning in August and was likened to a loose woman who wandered in the night. It was said *he whetu nui a Parearau, he wahine karihika, he wahine tiweka* ('the great star Jupiter, an immoral woman, a wandering woman').

Tautoru the bird-hunter

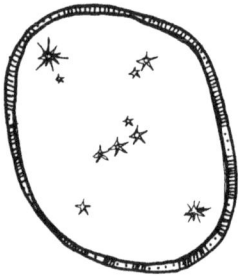

The constellation of Orion shines high in the sky, with Tautoru (Orion's Belt) clearly visible. There is a story about Tautoru. He was famous as a skilled bird-hunter, who used berries and sweet-smelling flowers to bait his snares. His specially trained dogs ran with him to catch the ground-dwelling birds kakapo, weka and kiwi. Too wise to rely solely on his skill, Tautoru invoked the support of Tane, god of the forest, through karakia and rituals. Even though he was only a mortal, Tautoru was so skilful and strong that Rauroha, a goddess of the air, fell in love with him. Every night she descended from the sky to stay with him until dawn, but always she hid her face. Tautoru longed to see it, even though he knew this was forbidden. One night his longing to see Rauroha's beauty became so great that he broke the tapu and gazed upon her as the dawn light flooded over her beautiful features. Rauroha fled instantly, leaving Tautoru grief-stricken at losing her. He was so distraught as he went about his work of snare-setting that he slipped from a tall tree and fell to his death.[14]

Rauroha saw birds wheeling about the tree top, crying out, and descended to find Tautoru lying on the ground. She sent a message for his kin to come and get his body, which they did; but as they were carrying the stretcher home they noticed that it had become very light. When they looked, they found to their amazement that his body had disappeared. The tohunga later explained to them that because of Tautoru's observances to Tane, Tane the first bird-snarer must have taken him up into the heavens. From that time he has remained there as the star cluster that bears his name and forms the shape of a bird snare. Jauntily rising out of the snare is the star Puanga (whose appearance announced winter solstice) which was seen as the pewa, the flower decoy that attracts birds. And if you look closely, you will also see the flocks of tiny kereru flying to be caught.[15]

Pagan Europe

Celtic society

In the old Celtic calendar the name for First Light was Imbolg, or Imbolc, derived from the older word Oimelc or Oi-melg, the Celtic word for ewe's milk. After the cold of winter the flowing of milk was significant, not only to nourish new lambs, but for old people and the very young. For them the availability of milk could mean the difference between life and death, especially as the weather was still cold. At Imbolc milk was poured on to the earth as an offering.[19]

This was regarded as the beginning of spring, marked by the lighting of fires and rituals to bless the coming crops. It was time to celebrate the return of the Goddess in her maiden aspect, released from the tower where she had been held by the Cailleach (pronounced the same as the Indian goddess Kali[20]), or crone aspect of the Goddess. This was a time of women's rituals, celebrating the Goddess and the mystery of her return.

And frosts are slain and flowers begotten, And in green underwood and cover Blossom by blossom the spring begins. (Swinburne, 'Atalanta in Calydon')[16]

The racing lambs too have fair their fling. (Gerard Manly Hopkins, 'Spring')[17]

Brigid, Brigid, won't you come in?[18]

Ancient Greece

Rituals of renewal also took place in ancient Greece at this time, with the lesser Eleusinian Mysteries being celebrated at Agrae near Ilissus in honour of the return of the maiden Persephone from the underworld and her reunion with her mother Demeter. The ritual was an important prerequisite to the greater Mysteries that took place at autumn equinox.

Fire symbolism

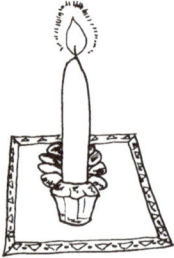

The lighting of candles or torches is a feature of many of the First Light rituals. In the lesser Mysteries it was a torchlight procession that took place at night; for the Romans it was the burning of candles in a purification ritual dedicated to Juno Februa, mother of Mars.[21] In ancient Britain, at the neolithic site of Avebury, the Feast of Lights was celebrated at this season. People carried torches at night to help the Goddess return from the underworld and be born again.[22] In the Celtic women's festivals of Imbolc, candles or torches were lit at midnight. Later the use of fire would survive in the post-Christian tradition of burning the Christmas decorations at First Light, 40 days after Christmas.[23]

Brigid

First Light belonged to Brigid, goddess of the Celtic empire of Brigantia, which once covered parts of Spain, France and Britain. One of her earliest shrines was at Brigeto in the Balkan Peninsula. Daughter of the Celtic god the Dagda, she had two sisters also called Brigid, one associated with healing and one with smith-craft. They were known as the 'three mothers' or 'the three blessed ladies of Britain' and were associated with the moon in its three phases, waxing, full and waning: Maiden, Mother and Crone.

It was Brigid in her maiden aspect who became associated with First Light. She represented the power of the new moon, spring and the flowing sea. In pagan times her statue was washed annually in the sea or a lake, signifying renewal, and she was greeted with candles and water.[24] The cow was associated with Brigid because of its nourishing milk, and the cauldron of plenty was one of her symbols.[25] Her flower was the sun-yellow dandelion, whose white juice suggested milk and was thought to nourish young lambs.[26]

Brigid was strictly a women's festival. In the Scottish Highlands the women would bar the door of the feasting house to the men, who had to plead humbly to be allowed to honour Bride.[27]

Fertility rites were part of the Celtic celebrations of Brigid or Bride, where the women dressed a sheaf of corn in female clothing. It was then placed in a basket with a phallic-like club and called 'the bride's bed'. The basket was put on to a bed of hay or corn, and candles lit all around it so that the 'bride' could be invited to come to it. Just before going to bed the women would cry out three times, 'Bride is come. Bride is welcome.' In the morning they would examine the ashes of the fire for an impression of Bride's club, which would be greeted as an omen of a good crop and a fertile year to come.[28] The practice is suggestive of even more ancient rites, where the coupling of a man and woman was thought to encourage crop fertility.

Sometimes the dressed straw doll or 'brideog' was taken from house to house in procession, or a chosen girl dressed in white would be taken around instead. Cakes, butter and other food would be laid out for this impersonation of Brigid.[29]

Another custom that lives on in the British Isles is the making of Brigid-crosses from straw or corn, their shape being either the goddess lozenge or the four-armed swastika known as the fire wheel. As a fire goddess, her cross was seen as protection against fire or lightning. In Ireland her festival was regarded as the first day of spring, and the time to prepare for the sowing of crops. In some places farmers would remove their trousers and sit on the bare ground to test whether it was warm enough to plough.[30]

In the Scottish Highlands Feill Bhride (Gaelic for St. Bride's Day) was celebrated at the beginning of February. It was a sign that winter was turning and spring was on its way. The raven, an important harbinger of the end of winter, was watched for weather prospects and referred to in the old Celtic saying:

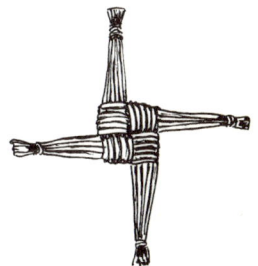

On the Feast Day of beautiful Bride
The flocks are counted on the moor
The raven goes to prepare its nest.

It was also said: *Fitheach moch, feannag anmoch* ('the raven [in voice] early, the hooded crow late'), the raven's early appearance signifying fine weather to come. Another sign of Feill Bhride was the opening of 'the little notched flower of Bride', the golden-yellow dandelion.[31]

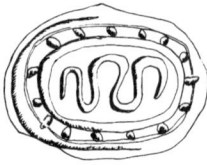

In the Scottish Highlands it was said that a snake emerged from the hills on the day of Bride. People made snake effigies on this day in honour of emerging life.[32]

Christian Europe: Candlemas

Saint Brigid

In early Christian Ireland there was a saint who took her name from the goddess and inherited Brigid's essential characteristics. Her story illustrates the vitality of the pagan tradition in Ireland and its resistance to Christian colonisation. The myths that grew up around Saint Brigid told of her birth at sunrise, neither in nor outside a house. She was said to have been fed by the milk of a white, red-eared cow, recalling both the milk of Imbolc and the significance of the colour red, which for the Irish was charged with supernatural powers. The cow was, of course, the companion animal of her pagan namesake. Brigid, they said, hung her wet cloak on the rays of the sun, and wherever she stayed, that house would appear to be ablaze with fire. With 19 of her nuns she was said to guard a sacred fire that never went out, a fire that was enclosed by a hedge within which no man was permitted to enter.[33] The number 19 is a reflection of the 19-year cycle of the Celtic Great Year, 19 being the number of years it took for the new moon to coincide with winter solstice once more.[34]

Despite the efforts of Christianity to overcome the goddess tradition, Irish writers persisted in referring to Saint Brigid as 'Queen of

Heaven', an echo of her older forms as Juno Regina and Tanit the Heavenly Goddess.

Brigid was associated with both fire and the underground, and many sacred wells – 'Bride-wells' or 'St Bride's wells' – were dedicated to her, and visited at festival time for purification. The Irish shamrock with its three leaves was said to stand for her three aspects.[35] The Church over-rode this by claiming the four-leafed clover was superior, and a sign of good luck. To this day, Irish people visit sacred wells and leave signs there, from handkerchiefs and glasses to asthma inhalers and tampons, in the hope of receiving healing.

Candlemas

Later, the Church transformed the festival of Brigid into the Feast of the Purification of the Virgin, or Candlemas, marking the time when Mary completed her ritual cleansing after the birth of Jesus and brought him to Jerusalem for blessing. Candlemas, with its burning of candles at midnight, retained much of the pagan symbolism of fire and cleansing. In the north of England it was called 'The Wives' Feast Day', acknowledging its earlier origins as a women's fertility festival. Later it became the traditional time for the more secular custom of spring-cleaning.

Weather predictions

In Britain the weather at First Light, or Candlemas, was thought to be a significant portent of the season to come, and rhymes abound to this effect. Many of them carry the theme that a fine clear day at Candlemas is a sign of a prolonged winter, but a cloudy or rainy day means spring is not far away:

> If Candlemas Day is fair and clear
> There'll be two winters in one year
> (trad. Scottish)

> If Candlemas Day be wind and rain

Winter is gone and won't come again
(trad. Warwickshire)

If Candlemas Day be sunny and warm
Ye may mend your ault mittens and look for a storm
(trad. Cumbrian)[36]

If Candlemas Day be fair and bright
Winter will have another flight
But if Candlemas Day be clouds and rain
Winter is gone and will not come again![37]

The belief that Candlemas was an important time to foretell the weather for the coming season is found in the practice of watching the hibernating hedgehog or badger, one that continued through the Middle Ages. The hedgehog was supposed to emerge from its underground burrow for the first time on this day. If the sun was shining, however, the hedgehog might catch sight of its shadow and be scared back underground for another six weeks, encouraging winter to linger on. If the weather was cloudy, all would be well and the animal could safely stay above ground, letting everyone know that spring was near. In the United States this day is now observed as Groundhog Day.[38]

Lupercalia

As a postscript, it is worth noting the existence of a second festival, two weeks later, that was held in Rome. Called the Lupercalia, it too was a candle-lighting festival, held in honour of Proserpina's return from the underworld and reunion with her mother Ceres (the Roman names for Persephone and Demeter). The date of this festival, 14 February, was later taken over by the Church and named after the little-known St Valentine. St Valentine's Day, when lovers declare their passion, remains today as an echo of the fertility rites of Brigid. As Ophelia remarks of Valentine's Day in *Hamlet*: 'young men will do't if they come to't.'

Rituals for today

Why should we celebrate the 2 August festival of First Light? One reason is that it tunes us into the subtle movement of the seasons. If we do this, we become aware of the increasing light at this point midway between winter solstice and spring equinox, and we honour the delicate moment of first quickening. First Light is not so much a time for big festivals as for small, intimate gatherings, especially of women.

For this is the return of the Goddess as Maiden, released from her dark Crone phase, renewed once more as part of the cycle of birth, growth, death and rebirth. In welcoming her back from the underworld we celebrate renewal both in nature and in our own lives. The colour white signifies this phase of the Celtic triple goddess (black being the Crone phase and red the Mother phase). The white of the waxing moon, of candles, and of the newly flowing milk all reflect the Goddess in her Maiden aspect.

Maiden energy may be celebrated with a naming of goddesses of fire and of the dawn, of air and of light: Hine-ahu-one, Brigid, Mahuika, Rauroha, or the Maidens returned from the underworld: Persephone, Proserpina, Kore. Young girls may be remembered and blessed at this time, or invited to the rituals. Sweet-smelling spring flowers such as daffodils, jonquils, and snowdrops could be added to the circle or altar, and images of new-born lambs and any other symbols of delicate young life. Dandelions may be included to invoke the sun and the goddess Brigid.

Ritual food for First Light would be anything made of milk: milk puddings, yoghurt, white cheeses, as well as whitebait fritters, this being the inanga season. A traditional European Imbolc drink called 'lambswool' might be served. This is made by heating pieces of baked apple in wine, beer or cider with honey, spices and cream to make a frothy, white mixture that reminded people of lambs' wool. The following recipe comes from the court of Charles I: 'Boil three pints of ale; beat six eggs, the whites and yolks together; set both to the fire in a pewter pot; add roasted apples, sugar, beaten nutmegs, cloves and ginger; and, being well brewed, drink it while it is hot.'[39]

In women's ritual circles celebrating the Goddess, Brigid is the name given to the First Light ritual. It is welcomed as an opportunity to let go of any vestiges of winter and move forward into the increasing light. One way of doing this is to mark sticks of wood with signs representing anything that needs to be relinquished, and for people to throw them into the fire in an act of sacrifice to the transformative powers of Brigid and Mahuika the fire goddesses. Everyone then sits in a circle and sings 'Purify and heal us', a repeating chant that invokes cleansing (see songs and chants p. 196). Symbols and stories of Brigid and other fire goddesses might be shared, and also poems, for Brigid was the goddess of inspiration and poetry. Then comes time for inner contemplation: a bowl of milk might be passed as a symbol of the old Celtic Imbolc, and as each person gazes into it they tune in to whatever is seeking to emerge in their life. As this is identified and named, they light a candle in recognition of the increasing light and energy that supports the growth of new life, and the bowl is passed on.

In Europe, corn dollies and crosses were made to signify Brigid and the wheel of the sun. Here in Aotearoa where we raise animals rather than grain, the milk that flows for new lambs and calves may well be a more appropriate symbol to use in our rituals, remembering too that Imbolg meant 'ewe's milk' and that the cow was a symbol for the nourishing powers of the goddess Brigid.

To incorporate more elements of Aotearoa, a First Light ritual might begin with a dawn sighting of Kopu (Venus) or Parearau (Jupiter) on the horizon. Tautoru could be greeted, high in the sky, and the story told of the great bird-snarer who gazed on the face of the air goddess and subsequently fell from the tree-tops to his death, thus bringing the bird-snaring season to an end. The moment of changeover, from the forest-hunting season to the time of the land crops, the domain of Hine-raumati, could be marked by replacing a symbol of a forest bird, the kereru maybe, with seeds to represent germination. Alternatively, a rangiora leaf might be turned over to reveal its white underside, to welcome the return of the light. Rangiora leaves were waved by Maori dancers as a symbol of life.[40]

In both cultures there is a movement from dark to light, whether it be of the journey from the underworld to the world above, or from the

dark depths of the forest to the open land of the cultivation fields. The rituals created in either cultural context could be used to celebrate this movement of energy and encourage awareness of it.

1. Brougham, p. 120.

2. Frame, *The Pocket Mirror*, p. 54.

3. Simmons, p. 15.

4. Best, *Time*, p. 22

5. Best, *Time*, p. 19, and *Agric*, p. 216.

6. Makereti, p. 260.

7. Makereti, pp. 241-242.

8. Brougham, p. 120.

9. Brougham, p. 75.

10. Sidgwick, p. 54.

11. Riley, 2-12.

12. Best, *Time*, pp. 22-23 and *Astron*, pp. 27 and 63.

13. Best, *Astron*, p. 46.

14. There is a proverb that refers to the hazardous nature of the bird-snarer's work when he has to climb high trees: *he toa piki rakau he kai na te pakiaka* ('a brave person who climbs trees is food for their roots'); Brougham, p. 22.

15. Reed, pp. 202-203.

16. Hayward, ed., p. 376.

17. Hayward, ed., p. 387.

18. Old folk saying.

19. Gimbutas, *Language*, p. 110.

20. The Cailleach has much in common with the Indian goddess Kali. Both are associated with death and destruction; see Walker, *Dict*, p. 104 and p. 161.

21. Durdin-Robertson, p. 41.

22. Sjoo, pp. 33-34.

23. Cooper, p. 42.

24. Durdin-Robertson, p. 36.

25. Stewart, p. 109.

26. Gimbutas, *Language*, p. 110.

27. Durdin-Robertson, p. 40.

28. Frazer, *Bough*, p.177.

29. Cooper, p. 43.

30. Slade, p. 59.

31. Gordon, p. 59.

32. Gimbutas, *Language*, p. 135.

33. MacCana, p. 34.

34. Edwards, p. 122.

35. Walker, *Dict*, p. 452.

36. Kightly, p. 66.

37. Holden, p. 13.

38. Dunkling, p. 51.

39. F. Muir, p. 51.

40. Graham, p. 30.

Spring Equinox

Eostre, Te Wha o Mahuru, Te Koanga

21 – 22 September

Ka tangi te wharauroa, ko nga karere a Mahuru.
('When the shining cuckoo calls it is the messenger of spring').[1]

Quick stepping though the chill September wind
Ruth Dallas, 'A Tea-shop'[2]

The clematis spreads her trumpet, the grass heads rattle
Ripely, drily...
James K Baxter, *Autumn Testament*[3]

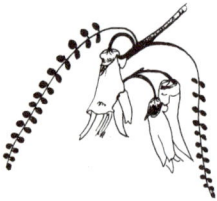

The exact moment of spring equinox usually comes in the morning, when light and dark are equal. From this moment the light begins to increase. Along stream beds and roadsides yellow kowhai flowers drip from the trees, attracting tuis to gurgle and grow fat on the sweet nectar. The first drifts of white manuka blossom swathe the hillsides, and in gullies the startling white of puawananga (clematis) leaps out from dark green bush foliage. Purple tutu is in flower, and dark red karo blossom sends out its rich fragrance into the night air. Whauwhaupaku (five-finger) fruit hangs in black clusters, attracting tui and tauhou (silvereyes). Far away the sound of a pipiwharauroa (shining cuckoo) is heard, and riroriro (grey warblers) trill from unseen places.

In the garden, blue and lilac flowers of borage, lavender and rosemary attract eager bees. Forget-me-nots, irises, bluebells and cinerarias add to the blue and purple keynote. Magnolia opens its fragrant petals and small flower clusters of the broom-like Breath of Heaven add to the sweetness in the air. Oak trees are coming into leaf, together with silver birch. Grapefruit and lemons ripen on the trees. Hens have resumed laying. All of Nature is stirring and quickening into life.

Aotearoa

In ancient Maori society the rising of the star Aotahi (Canopus) announced the arrival of spring, together with the flowering of kowhai, rangiora and kotukutuku, the plants of the fourth lunar month spanning September and October.[4] Puawananga (clematis), now flowering, was regarded as one of the three first-born children of the stars Rehua (Antares) and Puanga (Rigel). Its blossoming indicates the coming of spring, and it was believed to be created for this purpose.[5] The word puawananga contains pua (flower) plus wananga ('conspicuous' or 'associated with ritual and lore'); thus it means 'the conspicuous flower', or 'the ritual flower'. Knowledgeable people watched the flowering of trees in order to predict the weather for the coming season. If trees flowered on the lower branches first, it would be a tau ruru, warm and bountiful, but if they flowered on the upper branches first, it would be a tau matao, cold and unproductive.[6]

The third lunar month, characterised by 'crouching over the fire' and 'scorched knees', passes into the fourth, Mahuru-Matawai, when *ka whakaniho nga mea katoa o te whenua i konei* ('all things of the earth now sprout'), and *kua pumahana te whenua, me nga otaota, me nga rakau* ('the earth has got some warmth, as have plants and trees').[7] The old people liked to feel the sun on their skin in spring and would lie against a takitaki (fence) saying the old proverb, *Ae! Nga ra o toru whitu* ('Yes! the sun from the third to the seventh months!'). The old song line *te ra o te waru* refers also to the sun, stating that it warms for eight months of the year (the other four being cold).[8]

Fish

Up the rivers have swum the young inanga (whitebait), known as children of Rehua (the summer star) under whose watchful eye they will continue their life cycle.[9] Fully developed fish also make their way up the rivers now: the grayling and the kahawai, which were greeted with great excitement. The flowering of kowhai is a sign that the fish are fat.[10] In one eye-witness account at Whanganui:

> ...the river is a scene of the greatest bustle and activity; every canoe is launched and hurried through the water with the greatest rapidity, while over the stern trail two or three lines with shining native hooks attached. At these the kahawai jump like salmon at a fly, and are hauled in ... and as each fish is thrown into the bottom of the canoe it is greeted with

shouts and cheers… On all sides canoes are dashing about…and on all sides there is mirth and excitement, songs, shouts and cheers.[11]

Birds

The koekoea (long-tailed cuckoo) calling out 'koia! koia!' ('dig! dig!') and the trilling of the riroriro (grey warbler) reminded people to awaken to the task of the season: preparing the ground for the kumara crop. It was hard work digging the earth with a ko (digging stick) and some people might be tempted to absent themselves. Proverbial sayings could be used to chide them: *I hea koe i te tangihanga o te riroriro?* ('where were you when the grey warbler was singing?') Or, *I whea koe i te tahuritanga o te rau o te kotukutuku?* ('where were you when the fuchsia tree began to put on its leaves?') referring to the spring greening of the only native deciduous tree.[12] The proverb *Koanga, tangata tahi; ngahuru, puta noa* ('at digging time, a single helper; at harvest one is surrounded') referred to the same tendency towards absence when the work was hard, as did the saying *Take raumati, whakapiri ngahuru* ('absent at planting, close by at harvest').[13] People examined the nest of the riroriro for signs of the forthcoming weather. If the entrance hole faced east, it would be a bad season with prevailing westerly winds; if the entrance faced north it would be a tau kuraraki, a benign season.[14]

Return of pipiwharauroa

A key event was the return of pipiwharauroa, the shining cuckoo, from its winter stay in Hawaiki, the legendary Pacific homeland of the Maori. The bird's name acknowledges its capacity for long-distance travel, for wharau means 'to journey' and roa means 'long'. *Ka tangi te wharauroa, ko nga karere a Mahuru*, said the proverb: 'when the shining cuckoo calls it is the messenger of spring',[15] and it is still a sign that many listen for. It was heard crying kui! kui! – 'no food! no food!' from the treetops, and indeed food was now short as the rua (storehouses) became depleted. As another proverb reminded people, *Ngahuru kai hangai, koanga kai anga ke* ('at harvest eat openly, in spring eat secretly'), for when food is short it is not good to show that

one is enjoying it in front of others. Later, when the weather got warmer, the cuckoo knew that all would be well and added the call whiti! whiti ora! – 'changing, changing to plenty'. This call was the sign of a good summer to come.[16]

An old story tells how Mahuru sent the pipiwharauroa from Hawaiki to tell the Maori people it was time to plant, but the bird arrived too early and the crops failed. One interpretation of this story is that it refers to the fact that people failed to plant kumara at the right time when they first arrived in Aotearoa because they had not yet adjusted to the different climate.[17]

Harvesting karengo, kina, aruhe and ti

The purply-black seaweed karengo would be gathered from the rocks now,[18] and this still happens throughout the country. It was also a good time to get kina (sea eggs). Digging was not confined to the kumara plots, for this was also a season for digging aruhe (fern root), which would be roasted for about four hours and dried and stored for its nutritious rhizomes, which were especially high in starch content in spring. Aruhe was a staple food available both wild and in cultivated grounds, where if the soil was rich the root would have plenty of starch content and less fibre. The men would dig the roots and carry them back to the village to be dried in the wind on storage platforms sheltered from the sun. After two weeks they would be sorted into different grades and stored. If properly dried, fern root could be kept for years. The roots were full of a starch similar in taste to arrowroot, and were often made into small, flat loaves.

Aruhe was said to have been born out of the union of Tane and Tutorowhenua, who was taken as his wife especially for the purpose. The god of the aruhe was Haumia, who was one of the many children of Rangi the Sky Father and Papa the Earth Mother.[19]

Cabbage tree was cultivated too, both the imported ti pore and the native ti para. The roots and stems were dug in spring, dried in the sun and cooked in huge umu ti (earth ovens) and later eaten at feasts. During the two days it took for the roots to cook, couples were not allowed to have intercourse; on the other hand, if a woman developed

a craving for ti, it was thought to be a sign that she had conceived.[20] Fern fronds could also be eaten now, a welcome food when other supplies were short.

Kumara planting

The appearance of the star Aotahi (Canopus) towards the south of the sky was a sign for kumara planting to begin, as was the flowering of the kowhai, the bursting into blossom of the kumarahou, or the appearance of a 'mackerel sky'. When clouds formed into furrows resembling the widely spaced rows of a kumara patch in the sky, it was a sign that the atua (gods) had begun planting, and that humans should follow their example.[21] The furrows are sometimes called tiriwa (planting in rows at wide intervals).

This was a significant moment in the Maori year: kumara was the staple crop, the one that had best survived emigration from warmer islands. Important pure (purification rituals) took place before the planting. In one district the people would gather in a house in the evening. There the tohunga brought two kits of seed kumara. He chanted an incantation while every person present would touch the kumara as the kit was passed around. This was believed to protect against any bad influences that might lie within the soil. The seed would then be taken and planted after first offering the shoots to Matariki (the Pleiades) with an invocation asking for a bountiful crop. Later, at harvest time, the kumara planted in the night ritual would be the first to be dug and offered to Rongomatane, the god of cultivated food.[22]

Rongo was also the male personification of the moon (Hina being the female form), and had even more power over the growing of crops than Tane, who was associated with the sun. This was the case in Babylon also, and may reflect the origins of Maori culture in warmer climates where the sun was less important, being more constant all year round. On the upper part of the digging implements was sometimes carved the crescent moon, a symbol of the fertilising power of Rongo. Planting would be done on certain nights of the moon: the twenty-eighth night, i.e. dark of moon, or the fourth or eleventh nights of the waxing moon being auspicious times. The seventh, eighteenth or nineteenth might also be used.

Pani-tinaku

The deity of the kumara crop itself was the goddess Pani-tinaku, also known as Tinaku or Hine-tinaku. Tinaku meant 'to increase', and she was seen as the germinator, whose stomach was the storehouse. The innovation of storage was a vital development that allowed the Maori to subsist all year round in a land where kumara growth ceased in winter. The myths told of Pani giving birth to the kumara tubers in water, invoking her own powers as she did so: 'Oh Pani! Oh Pani! the germinator…they come down my aro' (birth canal):

> E Pani E! E Pani E!
> Opeope ki te Wai o Mona-ariki
> Ka heke i tua, ka heke i waho, ka heke i taku aro
> Me ko wai, me ko Pani.
> (Pani, Pani,
> Bathe in the waters of Mona-ariki
> [the kumara] descends behind, it descends outside,
> it comes down my birth canal,
> Who am I? I am Pani.)[23]

The water birth which bears little relation to the actual kumara planting in dry ground, may have its origins in deeper Maori ancestry in South-east Asia and Pani as goddess of the rice crop, for pani is a variant form of pari or vari, both South-east Asian names for rice.[24] In modern Hindi, pani means 'water'.

In a Tuhoe version of the myth, Pani was said to be one and the same as Taranga,[25] and that she adopted the name Pani when she entered the water in order to give birth to the kumara. Another interesting link is that Pani's husband was Rongo-maui, the younger brother of the star Whanui (Vega). Rongo stole the first seed tubers from Whanui in a daring raid, making it possible for Pani to give birth to them year after year.[26]

Planting rituals

The tohunga, walking about the kumara fields at the spring planting, would chant a long incantation to Pani, which included the following:

O Pani! O! Come hither now, welcome hither!
Fill up my basket...
Pile up my basket to overflowing,
Give hither, and that abundantly...[27]

Many important planting rituals took place in the different tribal areas. The men would dig in unison, in a line, while the tohunga chanted karakia. Digging was so characteristic of this season that spring is often called te koanga ('the digging'). Women were not allowed to make the mounds, or to dig, plant or harvest the kumara, but only to weed and cook it when it had been taken from the storehouses. Only a woman past menopause was permitted to enter the storehouses and remove the tubers.

The planting season began in September and might continue to November, with different varieties of kumara being planted in sequence. Four stars provided important signs for the planting: Matariki (the Pleiades), Tautoru (the three stars of Orion's Belt), Puanga (Rigel) and Whakaahu (Castor). If they foretold a good season, then planting would begin in September, but if not it would be delayed for a month. The kumara would be planted in lines running east to west, with the sprouts facing east. Then, as the season advanced the sprouts would face further north, reaching due north by the end of the planting season, thus following the course of the sun.

Amongst the Kahungunu tribe a captive miromiro bird (tit) was released to act as a messenger to the gods and obtain the mana for a good crop.[28]

Ritual planting often preceded the main planting. It would be done in a separate piece of ground called the mara tautane, set aside to be blessed by the gods. Each whanau (family group) offered a few seed tubers to be planted while karakia were chanted by men holding small green branches of mapou. Later these were stuck into the toropuke (earth mounds). The tapu was lifted and a ceremonial feast was held.

In the Waiapu district each person or family in the hapu (sub-tribe) gave two seed tubers for the totowahi (sacred kit), which was put at the edge of the field and covered with chickweed. Next morning mounds were formed and planting began. Food was cooked in a cere-monial umu called the unuunu. While the tohunga chanted karakia, he took the sacred kit and placed a kumara on each mound.[29]

In the South Island tohunga came to the kumara plantations in spring to dedicate them to Pani and Marihaka, the two kumara deities. Beginning in the left-hand corner of each plot, they put sprigs of koromiko in the ground and walked in a straight line to the other side, chanting karakia as they went.[30] At the top of each plot they gathered a handful of leaves or pitau (shoots), which they took to the nearest taumatua (shrine), an enclosed plot of ground known as 'the gods' garden' where four mounds were made and planted with kumara.

In some areas a carved stick or stone image would be placed on the east side of the kumara field. This was the mauri, the spirit of life, that would aid the growth of the crops. A green branch of mapau might be used for the same purpose. For the Arawa tribe, Matuatonga the kumara god was the mauri of the cultivations. He helped the crops to grow, the stored tubers to last, and protected the fields from evil influ-ences.[31] Once the pure had been completed the tapu was lifted. In Taranaki this song to the cuckoo would be chanted as a karakia while the men dug the ground:

Tangi te kawekawea – waiho kia tangi ana!
Tangi te wharauroa – waiho kia tangi ana!
E tatari atu ana kia aroaro-mahana, ka taka mai te ahuru!
Koia!

('The long-tailed cuckoo sings – let it sing!
The shining cuckoo sings – let it sing!
They are waiting for the summer, when the warmth will come!
Dig!)[32]

Parearohi

At spring equinox the first signs of the heat-shimmer of summer might be glimpsed, in the form of the goddess Parearohi. The word *arohirohi* means 'shimmering heat', and Pare was a common name for women, used as a prefix. One Maori informant described her in this way: 'In the fourth month this woman, Parearohi, who is a supernatural being, appears dancing about the margins of forests. Such is the first sign of summer, and when you see that strange sight you know that it is Parearohi dancing as summer approaches.'[33]

Pagan Europe

Eostre

Summer is a coming-in
Then loudly sing, cuckoo
(Old English poem)

Rise and put on your foliage,
and be seen
To come forth, like the Springtime, fresh and green.
(Robert Herrick)[34]

In Europe spring equinox was the festival of Eostre, the Saxon goddess of the dawn and spring. It was time to celebrate the new surge of growth after the dearth of winter. Eostre relates to German *ost*, meaning east, the direction of the rising sun, and *oster*, meaning 'to rise'. The old European custom of climbing a high hill before dawn at Easter to see the rising sun reflects both these meanings, as does the custom of 'lifting' or 'heaving' where men and women would lift a partner of the opposite sex into the air three times at Easter and then kiss them, an Easter practice that continued until the 12th century.[35]

Eostre was one of the most honoured Teutonic goddesses and for the Germans, Franks and Anglo-Saxons the month after equinox was Eostre month. Later, the full moon after equinox would become the Christian festival of Easter.

Little is known of Eostre, although she is believed to be related to the goddess Ishtar/Astarte. The Moon Hare, which the Celts saw in the full moon much as we now see a 'man in the moon', was her totem animal and the Easter lily her flower. The Moon Hare had ancient Indo-European origins; in Sanskrit the moon was known as *cacin*, 'that which is marked by the hare'. The hare was a sacred animal for the Celts, and was taken by Queen Boudica[36] as her totem animal, appear-

ing on her banners. Just before she led her famous rebellion against the Romans, Boudica released a hare from the skirts of her dress, in a dramatic gesture to divine a favourable outcome to the battle.

Eggs

The hare was said to lay eggs for good children, the egg being a symbol associated with the Goddess from ancient times as the sacred container of all creation. Eggs had almost universal significance throughout Europe and the Middle East. They were dyed bright colours and eaten at spring festivals in ancient Egypt, Persia, Greece and Rome. In Persia, spring equinox marked the beginning of the new year and coloured eggs were exchanged, a custom that continued to the middle of the 18th century. In many places, especially Eastern Europe, the eggs were dyed red, the colour of life blood, and in Greece today it is still the custom to place a red egg on a grave at Easter.[37]

The vegetation god

Throughout the Middle East and Europe, spring equinox rituals marked the resurrection of the god of vegetation who died in autumn. In ancient Egypt he was Osiris, murdered by his brother and hacked into pieces, then miraculously restored through the love of the grieving goddess Isis. Out of their union was born Horus, the sun god. In Sumeria he was called Tammuz, god of the grain, who was miraculously resurrected from the underworld by his lover the goddess Ishtar. His story was celebrated every spring in Jerusalem by the priestesses of Ishtar, who dramatically re-enacted Ishtar's mourning and Tammuz's resurrection, with the waving of palm branches to celebrate their reunion. His blood was said to fertilise the earth as he died, giving him the name 'son of the blood'.

In other cultures the same pattern was played out: the young god, often associated with the sun or agriculture, was sacrificed and sent to the underworld at harvest time, to be miraculously reborn in the spring, often through the intervention of his goddess lover. In Syria and Greece Tammuz became Adonis, and here again the earth was fertilised

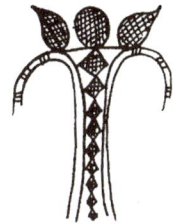

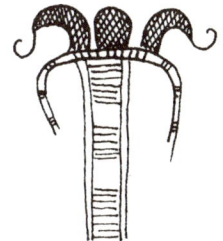

by the outpouring of his sacred blood as he died. From there it gave rise to the wild red flowers of *Anemone coronaria*, which flowered at spring equinox.[38] 'Gardens of Adonis' were grown in his honour to mark the return of the life-force. Women planted wheat, barley, lettuces, fennel and flowers in baskets or pots of earth and tended them for eight days. In Sicily women still sow gardens of Adonis, planting wheat, lentils and canary seed in plates, which are kept in the dark and watered every two days. The stalks of the shooting plants are tied with red ribbon, recalling the blood of the dying god. They are placed on sepulchres on Good Friday, recalling the ancient custom of offering the new shoots to the grave of the dead Adonis.[39] At Eleusis in Greece, sprouting kernels of grain were planted for Adonis in sacred pots called kernos, symbolising the womb of the goddess, and these continued to be planted by Italian women until the 20th century.[40]

Attis

In the ancient land of Phrygia near Cyprus, the young god was called Attis and his goddess lover, Cybele. The story of his resurrection spread to Rome, where it became central to the spring equinox festival. Attis, a vegetation god, died after the August harvest. Known as 'very fruitful' and 'the reaped green or yellow ear of corn', he embodied the spirit of growth. The story of his suffering, death and resurrection was also the story of the corn. In its ripeness it was cut down by the reaper, buried in the granary, to come miraculously to life again when sown at spring equinox.[41] In some versions of the story he was gored by a wild bull; in others he castrated himself, but in each case he bled to death under a pine tree. As he died his spirit passed into the tree, which was cut, bound with linen and decorated with spring violets. As it was brought into Rome on wagons the sorrowing people wept, with men or priests often cutting themselves with knives during the 'blood days' that followed. In older times self-castration was part of the blood-letting, and the priest who played the part of Attis may well have been killed himself as a sacrifice.

The practice of male ritual blood-letting has sometimes been interpreted as an imitation of women's menstrual bleeding, even an act of envy. (In terms of the life cycle of the Goddess, the Maiden reaches puberty at spring equinox and would be beginning to bleed, a suggestive parallel to the rites of Attis.) At equinox the vegetation god's spirit rose out of the pine tree to be reunited with that of his lover Cybele. Amid much happiness the garlanded tree was erected and the festival of Hilaria followed, ending on 1 April. This date was the carnival of the April Fool: Attis: Prince of Love. The festival spread throughout Europe and the resurrected tree became the maypole. At winter solstice, as mentioned previously, Attis's decorated pine tree formed the basis of our modern Christmas tree.

Such myths of the Goddess and the horned son/lover god come from the urban matriarchal period, when goddess spirituality was at its peak.

Mabon and other saviour gods

In Celtic society spring equinox was the 'time of winds'. The young god was Mabon, the divine child of light, who had been imprisoned in a dark dungeon since he was three years old. At spring equinox, following the call of the men of the hunt, he was released.

Other young 'saviour' gods were Orpheus and Dionysus. To Carl Jung the myths spoke of the need for the young male initiate to abandon himself to his instinctual nature and thus be open to the full, replenishing, fertilising power of the Earth Mother.[42]

The fertility gods came only for a season, being born of the Mother and sacrificed back to her, to be resurrected and reunited with her as her lover in the spring. Like the green, upward-shooting sap the Green God rose annually from the holding power of the earth, the Great Goddess herself.

Christian Europe: Easter

Christianity did its best to override the pagan rituals, but the cyclical fertility rites had taken too great a hold on people's consciousness.

Finally, the Church included many of the elements of the older rites: the raising of the cup of blood (wine) which was a gesture of sacrificial offering to the Goddess (God). The passion of Christ was arbitrarily attached to 25 March, the Roman festival of the vegetation god Attis. Thus the death and rebirth of the Saviour were linked with a long-standing tradition of the sacrifice and resurrection of the young god, which in turn was linked to the autumn/spring cycle of death and regrowth.

Easter came to be celebrated on the first full moon after spring equinox, a tradition based on the old lunar calendar. It remains the only shifting festival in our present-day system; despite attempts to fix it to one date, Easter stays tied to the moon. The full moon was the pregnant phase of Eostre, and in the late Middle Ages the Christian festival came to be called Easter, reflecting the season of rebirth in the cycle of the goddess.

Eostre's moon-hare lives on in the diminished form of the Easter bunny. Hot-cross buns recall the sacred cakes once made of fine flour and honey that were offered to the goddess and were known as boun.[43] Boun means 'sacred ox', and refers to the practice of sacrificing an ox at spring equinox. The cross represents a stylised version of ox horns, which links it with early moon worship also.[44] The cross has also been linked to Wotan's cross, the phallic tree-of-life symbol.[45]

Rituals for today

Spring equinox (21/22 September) is the true place for the Easter rituals, and if Easter were to be held now it would be a time full of reminders of rebirth and the greening of hope. The resurrection of Christ would be connected with the resurrection of the Green Man, and together with the rising sap would become part of an all-inclusive celebration.

Even without the transposition of Easter to its true time in the seasonal cycle, spring equinox carries many meanings. In the agricultural cycle of Aotearoa, this was te koanga, the digging and planting time. It was a season of hard work. Even though fresh green shoots sprouted forth from the kumara tubers in response to spring energy, the participation of human beings was necessary for those shoots to grow and develop.

Spring equinox rituals could be a time for people to gather outside around a patch of earth. Here each person would take a trowel and turn or dig the earth in honour of te koanga, the digging. Maybe the sound of the pipiwharauroa crying 'kui! kui!' and the koekoea crying 'koia! koia!' could be listened for, as well as the trilling of the riroriro. The birds give the signal to begin the ritual. As each person turns the earth they are invited to reflect on the value of the hard 'digging' work that we do in order to prepare ourselves for new growth.

After the digging could come the symbolic seeding of the earth. Each person is given a seed or handful of seeds. As they hold them in their hands they contemplate what quality, action or new attitude they wish to plant in their lives. What is it that lies within them in seed form, awaiting the right conditions for growth? We might contemplate what hopes or projects we are planting now, knowing that no matter what may have died in us over the winter, we can be reborn and grow anew, supported by the quickening energy of the season. The participants each name what they are seeding, and then place the seeds in the newly turned earth. Another possibility would be to plant seeds into small pots, recalling the 'Gardens of Adonis' of early Greece.

The rituals would also acknowledge the supportive energies for the growing season: Rongomatane, the god of cultivated foods, to bless the crops; and Pani-tinaku, the goddess who goes into water to give birth to the kumara crop every year, a sacred event to be aware of and to honour, for the kumara was to the Maori what the corn was to the European, the basic crop of life.

The young green god Attis/Adonis/Osiris, who rises from the dead corn as fresh new shoots every spring, could also be greeted.

Eggs may be dyed many colours and exchanged to symbolise the joy of rebirth: onion skins give an orange colour, and cochineal red. Designs may be drawn on with a wax crayon before dyeing, perhaps using the old markings of the Goddess: the zigzag, wavy lines, or the lozenge. A basket of brightly dyed and decorated eggs could be placed

in the centre of the ritual circle. Coloured boiled eggs may form part of the ritual feast, together with other traditional foods of the season, such as karengo and aruhe. Sacred cakes or buns ('boun') with the cross of Wotan the tree god imprinted on them could be eaten as part of the celebrations, and the hare honoured as Eostre's totem animal, representing fertility.

Flowers are abundant at spring equinox and may form an important part of the ritual setting. The colour red may be a keynote, to assert the power of the life blood. It could be included in the form of karo flowers, red poppies, red anenomes or tulips, contrasting with the white of manuka. This is an ideal time to celebrate the menstruation of young women, for in the life cycle of the Goddess spring equinox is when the Maiden is about to become Woman. Eostre, goddess of spring and of the dawn, presides over the awakening of the Maiden into a new phase.

For some old Easter carols, consider 'Easter Eggs'[46] , 'Hilariter'[47] or 'Love is Come Again'.[48] For a simple chant for this land, try

> The kowhai and the cuckoo
> Sing to my heart
> And the clematis is weaving
> Through the winds of spring.
> (See songs and chants p. 196)

Greenery and new growth may be used to symbolise the return of the vegetation god. We might greet him as the Green Man in the hope that this old archetype will once more be born to the earth, signifying as it does the association of male energy with the greening forces of nature. The Green Man could be seen as the necessary counterpart to 'Mother Earth'. Men might identify with him by dressing in green, or wearing greenery in the spring rituals, and by doing so find inspiration for their vital role in the restoration and conservation of the planet.

1. Brougham, p. 110.

2. Curnow, ed. p. 249.

3. Baxter, p. 34.

4. Best, *Time*, p. 27.

5. Best, *Forest*, p. 33.

6. Best, *Forest*, p. 33.

7. Best, *Time*, p. 27 and p. 19.

8. Beattie, p. 46.

9. Best, *Astron*, p. 43.

10. Dell Wihongi, pers. comm.

11. Best, *Fishing*, p. 41.

12. Brougham, p. 65.

13. Mitchell, pp. 245-247 (Ngati Kahungunu).

14. Best, *Forest*, p. 330.

15. Brougham, p. 110.

16. Best, *Forest*, p. 339.

17. Best, *Agric*, p.145.

18. MacDonald, p. 130.

19. Makereti, p. 203.

20. Riley, 9-2.

21. Best, *Agric*, p. 184.

22. Barlow, p. 102.

23. Best, *Agric*, p. 106.

24. Best, *Agric*, pp. 102-103.

25. The goddess who gave birth prematurely to Maui-potiki and put him out to sea floating on the topknot of her hair. See Grace & Kahukiwa, p. 72.

26. Best, *Agric*, p. 102.

27. Best, *Agric*, p. 107.

28. Best, *Agric*, p. 146.

29. Best, *Agric*, pp. 156-157.

30. For the texts of two Kahungunu planting karakia, see Mitchell, pp. 236-237.

31. Makereti, pp. 180-181.

32. Orbell, *Poetry*, pp. 76-77 and p. 100.

33. Best, *Astron*, p. 20.

34. Sitwell, Vol 1, p. 363.

35. Kightly, p. 105 and p. 191.

36. Fraser, p. 71, and Walker, *Dict*, p. 377. Boudica's name was later altered to Boadicea as she became a legendary figure.

37. Barz, p. 55.

38. Walker, *Dict*, p. 423, and Frazer, *Bough*, p. 433.

39. Frazer, *Bough*, p. 449 and p. 454.

40. Walker, *Dict*, pp, 150-151.

41. Frazer, *Bough*, pp. 464-465.

42. Jung, p. 141.

43. Durdin-Robertson, p. 64.

44. Brasch, pp. 43-44.

45. Walker, *Dict*, p. 483.

46. Easter eggs! Easter eggs!
Give to him that begs!

Those who hoard can't afford –
moth and rust their reward!

Easter tide, like a bride, comes, and won't be denied. (Dearmer, p. 204).

47. Dearmer, p. 206.

48. Now the green blade riseth from the buried grain;
Wheat that in the dark earth many days has lain;
Love lives again, that with the dead has been:
Love is come again, like wheat that springeth green. (Dearmer, p. 306).

FLOWERING AND SAP-RISE

Beltane, Whiringanuku

31 October

October 31 comes halfway between spring equinox and summer solstice. It is a high-energy time, when the whole earth sings of growth and regeneration. Birds are nesting, deciduous trees leafing, flowers are blossoming and the increasing sun power quickens both sap and blood.

The bush is now full of flowers, some very noticeable, and others less so, like the small blossoms of rimu, kahikatea, and karaka. High in the tall rewarewa emerge the velvety spikes of its deep red flowers, and at a lower level the yellow stars of korokio. Manuka flowering is prolific now and is greeted by the koekoea (long-tailed cuckoo) with a cry of 'Hoi!' in recognition of the season. Kotukutuku is producing its reddish-purple fuchsia blossoms. Dark red flowers of karo hide under shoots of new, light green foliage, sending out their rich fragrance into the night air, and everywhere the bush is bright with the new season's greening. Koromiko, tutu, nikau, akatea and tataramoa bloom, along with the feathery fronds of toetoe and large, creamy heads of ti (cabbage tree). A good flowering of ti kouka is said by the Maori to be a sign that a long, fine summer will follow.

Rima ka kaukau ana tangata (The fifth month, when people swim again)

Aotearoa

To the Maori, this was Whiringanuku, the fifth month, when *kua tino mahana te whenua* ('the earth has now become quite warm'),[1] *ka whakaniho nga mea katoa o te whenua i konei* ('all things now put forth fresh growth')[2] and *rima ka kaukau ana tangata* ('people swim again').[3] The comment from Natanahira Te Hurupa of Ngati Huarere and Waiohua reminds us of the widespread contemporary custom among many New Zealanders of taking their first swim at Labour Weekend, in late October.

Fragrant plants: tarata, titoki and mairehau

Yellow-green tarata fragrance fills the air. The flowers were used as perfume by the Maori; after being combined with fat the whole mixture could easily be rubbed on to the body. Its leaves are as sweet as the flowers, giving off a lemon smell when bruised; hence its European name of lemonwood.[4] Along with kohuhu, tarata leaves were often used for bedding because of their fragrance. The Maori also used to extract resin, known as pia tarata, from the bark. It would be mixed with the juice of puha and rolled into a ball that was chewed to sweeten the breath. The gum was also used for scenting oil from the titoki berries.

Titoki is flowering. It too was made into perfume in the past, with both leaves and flowers becoming part of the scented oil. Sweet-smelling mairehau with its white, star-like flowers is also abundant now. Maori would rub their bodies with the young branches and make sachets from the fragrant leaves.[5]

In honour of such sweet scents, the Maori had a beautiful saying that was used as a form of endearment, especially to a small child:

taku hei piripiri	my pendant of scented fern
taku hei mokimoki	my pendant of sweet-scented fern
taku hei tawhiri	my pendant of scented gum
aku kati taramea	My sachet of sweet-scented speargrass.[6]

Hinau: the conception tree

The hinau tree is putting forth its droops of beautiful, white, bell-shaped flowers. It was a significant tree to the Tuhoe women, who would go to a special hinau known as Te Iho-o-Kataka, high on a bush ridge, to invoke help in conceiving a child. It was said that if they clasped the eastern side of the tree, where the morning sun shone, they would conceive a boy, and if they held the western side of the tree, a girl would be theirs.[7]

Stars

Whakaahu (Castor) continues to be visible in the night sky, along with Puanga (Rigel). Puanga was watched closely as an indicator of weather. Its early appearance in the northern sky was a sign that planting should begin, but if the star was late the season would also be late. Aotahi (Canopus) was also watched. If it stood apart from the Milky Way, the summer would be a dry one, but if Aotahi clung close bad weather would follow.[8]

Planting and digging

In the cultivation grounds, planting of kumara continued, and after European contact the ground would be prepared now for planting of the potato, a later crop that was easier to grow and store. Digging of fern root continued, and young fern fronds were picked for eating. The Tuhoe burned bracken on the tawaha aruhe (rhizome digging ground) to improve the quality of the roots, taking as their signal the flowering of hinau and tawari trees. The main digging was done just as the young fern fronds were put forth. If the burning and digging were left until the rata and korukoru flowered (more into summer), the rhizomes would not be so nutritious. In the Bay of Islands the fern-root digging season was much earlier, spanning May to July, due to the warmer weather. Although fern root was at its best in spring, it could be dug for most of the year, usually from April to October, hence the saying: *Ka ora karikari aruhe, ka mate takiri kaka* ('the fern-root

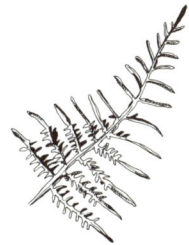

digger survives when the parrot snarer is in dire straits').[9] Aruhe was a prized food. After roasting and beating the roots were peeled and eaten, the starchy inner substance tasting rather like arrowroot. Aruhe was also made into small, flat loaves, or mashed with mata (whitebait) into a mixture known as kohere-aruhe.[10]

Harvest of the ti

Now that the kumara demanded less attention, it was time to go into the bush to cut the cabbage tree. In the South Island, where other food was scarce, the Ngai Tahu and Ngati Mamoe tribes cultivated both the imported ti pore and the native ti para and ate the roots and stems of the young plants. People moved to the sites and set up camp. The night before cutting began the tohunga lit a fire and chanted karakia while each person took their own kouka (cabbage tree leaves) or rito (flax shoot) and put the leaves on the fire, then took them off again at the right time. Each whanau (family group) did its own ritual, invoking both male and female elements.

The next morning the trees were cut and the bark chipped away. The inside of the trunks were set up on end to dry; the people then went home, and in the northern half of the South Island attended to the kumara planting.

Later they returned for a second felling of trees while the first cutting, now dry, was tied up in bundles and carried to the fires for steaming. Huge puna (pits) were dug for this, about two metres deep and 40 metres long. When the morning star rose fires were lit in the pits, and the trunks steamed on the heated stones for a night and a day. The kauau (pith) was then pounded and stacked on raised platforms to dry further.[11] Preparation of kauru, the resulting sago-like food, was strenuous work.[12]

This was a season of promise: a flowering and growing time as kumara plants spread their tendrils through the moist earth and flowers of the forest trees anticipated the fruiting season to come.

Pagan Europe

The Roman Floralia

In Europe the mid-spring festival was a time of high celebration. The Romans celebrated the flowering of nature in the festival of the Floralia, from 28 April to 3 May. It was held in honour of Flora, the goddess of spring, who was also the twin sister to Pan (Faunis). Pan was the mortal forest god who protected wild animals, bees and hunters. He took on both animal and human forms, with flashing green eyes and a hairy body. As the shepherd he held a crook, whose curved head suggests both animal horns and the moon. He played music on pipes and held a pine tree twig, a symbol pointing to his affinity with the vegetation god Attis.

His twin sister Flora presided over vines, fruit trees, grains and flowers that told the promise of fruit to come. At her festival people offered her flowers at springs and rivers, and let themselves go in the expression of sexual freedom. It was also an occasion for cleaning and purification of the temples – a forerunner of the surviving custom of 'spring-cleaning'.

The Roman Fontanalia

Associated with this was the Fontanalia, a festival dedicated to the spirits of the reviving waters. Girls and young women made garlands of corn and flowers to hang on doors. Houses, byres and stables were decorated with hawthorn, rowan, fir, birch or other greenery to keep evil spirits away. Flower garlands were thrown into waters. Springs and wells were decorated with flowers, a custom that carried over into Christian times; 'well-dressing' is still a custom in parts of England and Europe. Nearby bushes and trees were hung with ribbons or pieces of cloth, and for healing, a piece of the sick person's clothing would be hung there. Faeries and witches were said to be active at this season.[14]

Spring, the sweet spring, is the year's pleasant king;
Then blooms each thing, then maids dance in a ring,
Cold doth not sting, the pretty birds do sing -
Cuckoo, jug-jug, pu-we, to witta-woo.
(Thomas Nashe, 'Spring')[13]

Neolithic rituals

From ancient times this was recognised as the season of high sexual energy, and it was celebrated in uninhibited ways. The coupling of man and woman was a magical act that invoked the fertility of the earth and its power to bring forth new crops. It was a celebratory alignment of energies, a natural dialogue between human beings and elemental forces. At the neolithic site of Avebury in Wiltshire, young men and women are thought to have danced and wound their way along the serpentine avenues until they reached the Avebury Circle in the centre, where the communal ritual coupling took place. As part of the ceremony the whole community danced around the outer banks with their arms upraised in imitation of the horned new moon.[15]

Celtic Beltane

Great herds of deer once roamed over Britain. Their antlers that sprouted anew in April and grew rapidly through May and June had since ancient times been a metaphor for resurgent growth and renewal. Men identified with the deer in the Celtic Great Rite that was enacted to bring fertility to the land for the coming season. At the start of May, the Stag Lord, a boy who had been chosen at birth and had reached his fourteenth year, was brought to run with the 'deer', who were actually masked and horned men. He had to overcome the Great Stag and so win the honour of ritually mating with the Goddess, a young woman chosen at birth and trained to accept the destiny that awaited her on this day.[16]

The Celts called this festival Beltane (pronounced *Bail*-tin[17]), and together with Samhain (pronounced *Shah*-vin) it divided the year into two main phases. At Samhain, the dying time in late autumn, the faeries were said to return to their burial mounds, the sidhs (pronounced 'shee'), but at the seasonal shift of Beltane the veil between the worlds once more grew thin, allowing the faeries and spirits of the dead to re-emerge. Having done so, they attempted to enchant mortal people, but in most of the old stories they do not succeed. Light triumphs over darkness as the season moves forward towards summer, and the faeries must wait until Samhain to have their victory.

When in post-Christian times Celtic poets wrote down the mythic history of Ireland, Beltane was identified as the time when important invasions took place. The first was when Partholan, god of the dead, arrived and gave birth to the Partholanians. Later at Beltane pestilence came and wiped out the entire race in one week.[18] After two more invasions, the Tuatha de Danann were said to have arrived in the south-west at Beltane. A race of divine beings who were skilled in Druid lore and magic, they were said to be people of the goddess Danu, or Brigid.[19] Much later, Beltane was the occasion of the last arrivals, the Celts, who were known as the Sons of Mil or the Milesians.[20] Beltane may have been selected as the time of these mythic invasions because it represented the spring season of growth and change, or because in the life of the Celts it marked the opening of the season of warfaring, which spanned the warm months until Samhain.[21]

In the old Celtic Coligny calendar Beltane spanned the month of 'shoots show' and the 'time of brightness',[22] and signalled not only the raiding season, but also the time for hunting to begin. It was marked by the setting of the Pleiades.[23] This was when the cattle were released from their winter enclosure to roam once more in fresh, green pastures, and, as at Samhain, fires were lit. Bones were burned to make acrid smoke that would fumigate the cattle; hence the word bonfire, which comes from the original 'bone-fire'. As the animals were driven between smoky fires they were released from any parasites, disease or evil spirits that they might have harboured over winter. Cattle-purification ceremonies are still held today in Celtic communities in Ireland, Britain, France and northern Italy. Various place-names still tell of important sites of Beltane fires: Tullybelton ('Beltane Hill') in Perthshire, Tan-y-bryn ('Fire Hill') in Carmarthenshire, and several Tan Hills in north or west Britain.[24]

Beltane signalled the reappearance in the dawn sky of the Pleiades, which were greeted with dance dramas about death and resurrection, some of which live on today. In parts of Devon and Cornwall the Padstow Hobby Horse festival is enacted on May Day (the old Beltane), with a large, masked 'horse' bursting out of a stable and into the streets. The mask's striking red, black and white design reflects the

magical colours of old Europe. There is dancing and singing till night, when the 'horse' dies, to be born again the following May.[25]

Beltane was a fire festival, Beltane meaning 'bright' (Bel) plus 'fire' (tene, teine). It was held in honour of Bel, the Celtic god of light, known also as Belenos, whose name meant 'shining', or 'brilliant'. He looked after the health of cattle, and encouraged the crops to grow. Later Belenos became the Celtic Apollo, who had therapeutic attributes and was associated with thermal springs. The custom of visiting sacred wells and springs and decorating them with flowers reflects this healing aspect of Bel. On the Isle of Man and the Orkneys the sick used to circle the wells sunwise and drink from them to draw on their healing energies.

Beltane fires

Bonfires were a focal point of the rituals. People danced sunwise around the flames or leaped over them to purify and encourage increase. Sacrifices were made to Belenos, sometimes with the slaughter of sick beasts that had not weathered the winter well. People carried burning torches around the fields to invoke the sun. Often these rites included sexual intercourse to invoke fertility on the earth. In older times the Beltane rites held a more sinister note, for human sacrifice was demanded to propitiate the gods and ensure a fertile growing season. The sacrificial victim would be chosen when grain cakes were passed out, one of which would be marked with a black, charcoal thumb-print. The person who drew the charred, or 'carline', cake, would be sacrificed.[26]

Once the rituals were completed and the cattle driven out to spring pastures, the tribe was also able to leave the confinement of its winter quarters. It was a popular time for visiting and the release of pent-up energies in enthusiastic celebrations.[27] Big gatherings took place and major fairs were held at important sites, Mayfair in London being one of these.

Christian Europe: May Day

Later the Beltane festival of 30 April became known as May Eve, and the following day May Day. This month was named by the Romans after Maia, the virgin goddess of springs; in northern Europe she was known as Maj or Mai, the Maiden. The May Day rituals continued on or near the sites of the old Beltane fires; for example at an enclosure just above the head of the lusty Cerne Giant on a Dorset hillside, not far from the old Beltane shrine.[29]

May Day was still celebrated under Christianity, despite the disapproval of some Protestant reformers, and it was not until the puritanical reign of Oliver Cromwell in the latter half of the 17th century that May Day was officially banned. It was later reinstated by Charles II, when the maypoles rose again in a symbolic ceremony in London. Samuel Pepys called it 'the happiest Mayday that hath been many a year in England'.[30]

May Day was sanctioned by many of the monarchs, Henry VII going maying on various occasions, with a huge entourage of courtiers. On one early May morning they rode out and met 200 men dressed in green, wearing green hoods, and carrying bows and arrows. Their leader, called Robin Hood, then put on an impressive shooting display and took the company into arbours in the forest where they were served venison and wine and lavishly entertained.[31]

The Church accepted and even supported May Day celebrations. The congregation might move easily from a morning church service to the village green for dancing and feasting, and then back to evening church before dancing again at night. In the Roman Catholic Church May became Mary's month, a natural evolution from its associations with the virgin goddess Maia. The survival of a May morning church service at Tissington in Derbyshire at various well-heads, also speaks of the relationship between Church and ancient customs. There the local people make bright, mosaic pictures of fragments of flower, moss and berries stuck on to wet clay, and put them around the wells. Of course, the attitude of the Protestant reformers was another story, but more of that later.

And furth goth all the Court,
both most and lest,
To feche the floures fresh,
and braunche and blome;
And namly, hawthorn brought
both page and grome,
With fresch garlandes,
partie blewe and whyte...
('The Court of Love',
15th century)

There's not a budding Boy,
or Girle, this day,
But is got up, and gone to
bring in May.
(Robert Herrick, 'Corinna's
Going A Maying')[28]

May Day was a riotous festival in honour of the renewal of nature's energies, with the arrival of the cuckoo and flowering of the hawthorn's white blossoms being important signals for the season. Both bird and flowers were sexy signals, the cuckoo coming to be linked with infidelity and being 'cuckolded'. Many rhymes and songs were composed to both cuckoo and may, the name given to hawthorn blossom because of its strong association with this month. Its green leaves were used to make a vitamin-rich spring tonic that invigorated people after the poor fare of winter, but this was not the only reason may was said to be energising. May Day came to denote a type of celebration that could take place at other times, even as late as midsummer, which is when it is celebrated in Scandinavia. Cambridge University in England still holds a 'May week' in June.[32] Shakespeare's *A Midsummer Night's Dream* is very much an expression of this permissive energy, named by Theseus when he says of the lovers sporting in the woods: 'No doubt they arose early to observe the rite of May.'

The rite of May

And what was the 'rite of May'? All over Europe it was enjoyed, with many local variations. A typical May Day rite might have gone something like this: on May Eve the young people gathered, laughing, giggling, excited, ready to go a-maying in the woods. The oak was now coming into leaf, along with many other plants. The cuckoo could be heard singing through the branches. There was a restlessness in the blood as the young men and women smelt the yeasty perfume of the hawthorn blossoms (may). The disapproving Church called it arbor cupidatis ('the tree of desire'),[33] and indeed whether it was the hawthorn or simply the season, the eagerness of youth, or collective memories being triggered of old orgiastic rites, the visit to the woods was likely to turn into more than an innocent collecting of greenery. Many a young man and young woman were initiated into lusty love-making on that night.

The overt purpose was not forgotten. Greenery was cut: birch and hawthorn branches and a tall fir tree which would be the maypole, often called 'the rod of peace'.[34] The young people stayed out all night.

In the morning they reappeared with their greenery, singing

> We've been rambling all the night
> And sometime of this day
> And now returning back again,
> We bring a garland gay.[35]

With those 'garlands gay' they decorated the houses. Many an occupant would be surprised on awakening to find showers of greenery and flowers over the doors and walls, or even a slender young tree rising out of the ground in front of the dwelling. The bringing of trees is a survival of the pagan belief in the fertilising power of trees, and it is interesting that this is also the season when in Aotearoa Tuhoe women used to clasp the white-flowering hinau tree to invoke aid in conceiving a child.[36]

The maypole

The maypole was brought through the village in style, in a cart drawn by 20 yoke of oxen, each with a bright nosegay of flowers cheekily hanging from its horns. On the cart lay the maypole, a tall birch or pine tree stripped of all but its upper branches, bedecked with red and white ribbons and strips of cloth, flowers and herbs. White symbolised the linen winding-cloth of the dead vegetation god Attis, and red the life-giving blood that surged again at his rebirth. With great ceremony the maypole was taken to the village green. Horns were blown and loud instruments played as the procession wended its merry way. The maypole was erected, and all around it bowers, arbours and summer halls were set up, a whole fair of games and sports, including archery.[37] The morris dancers, dressed in white and wearing bells, would make their entry, and then both young and old would join in the circle dances held around the maypole, with everyone holding hands and singing as they danced.

This motif of dancing around a tree, pole, cairn, rice sacks or sugar cane stalks is repeated throughout the world by groups of people wishing to invoke the fertilising powers of nature.[38]

Victorian times saw a revival of the old customs. The long ribbons and plaited maypole dancing so familiar to us now are in fact a product of that revival, when new forms of dancing were invented.[39] John Ruskin is said to have been largely responsible for introducing the ribbon-plaiting dances and the crowning of a child Queen.[40] May Day lives on in Britain as Labour Day, which is a public holiday.

The traditional 'wearing of the green' for May Day reflected people's identification with the burgeoning earth. Some of the chants used phrases from old Druid chants or blessings, such as 'hip, hip, hooray!' and 'hey, nonny, nonny'.[41]

The May queen and king

An important part of the festivities was the choosing, not of the Victorian-style child queen, but the sexually ripe May Queen and King, to represent the Spring Goddess and the Horned God. The young man was often chosen by a physical test, such as climbing the maypole to retrieve food that had been tied to the top, or racing others to the pole. This practice survives today in the custom of men climbing the greasy pole at fairs. The winner gained the honour of becoming the May King or Green Man, known by different names in various parts of Europe: Green George, Father May, or, if a child were chosen, 'Little Leaf Man'. He was dressed from head to toe in greenery. At Ruten in Belgium the men dressed in ivy leaves, layered like the scales of a dragon, in order to take part in the May festivals. In England a chimney sweep wore a wickerwork cage covered in holly and ivy. He was crowned with flowers and ribbons and known as Jack-in-the-green, a vivid embodiment of the spirit of nature.[42] The Green Man lives on today in the character of Robin Hood, the benevolent outlaw of Sherwood Forest.

The young woman was chosen for her beauty. She became the goddess of spring, known as the May Queen, and was crowned and adorned with flowers. The old song 'Greensleeves' is a love poem to the May Queen:

Greensleeves is my delight

Greensleeves is my heart of gold[43]

In Southern Ireland the May Queen retained her title for a year, but lost it if she should marry during that time.[44] The modern beauty contest may owe its beginnings to these old customs, although it has become completely divorced from the original context where female beauty and maidenhood were celebrated as manifestations of the Goddess in her phase of renewal.

The presence of both the May Queen and the May King reflected a union of male and female 'greening' forces of youth, vigour and fertilising power. This was very different from the split that later evolved, leaving women as the sole representatives of 'Mother Earth'. We could well draw inspiration from the old May Day rituals today, for they offer a model for the integration of male and female 'green' values, celebrated with vigour and joy.

Rituals for today

Celebrating Beltane on 31 October gives us an opportunity to connect with the full, lusty growth of spring, the surging of our own plans and hopes, supported by the great growth spurt in nature.

The best place to celebrate Beltane is outdoors. We can gather flowers: karo, koromiko, rewarewa, and the fragrant mairehau, titoki and tarata as well as whatever the garden offers in the way of exotics. Early-flowering manuka might well be used as our equivalent to white may (hawthorn).

A Beltane ritual might focus on water, for healing waters were important at this time in the European tradition, and are also an important part of Maori ritual practice, where sacred water was used for healing, initiation, cleansing and to instil knowledge.[45] In both Maori and Pakeha culture it is time to take the first swim. We could make this a very conscious act at Beltane, by going on a journey or walking to some special healing waters, maybe a spring, a hot pool, or bush stream, and there making contact with the life-giving energy of

water and its power to renew us. For Beltane is a time to re-energise and connect with our vital force.

Fire is the second element to include at Beltane. We might light a bonfire at night and dance around it sunwise (which is anticlockwise in the Southern Hemisphere) or jump over it to banish old fears and inhibitions, especially around sexuality. Beltane is time to celebrate our sexual energy, or to invoke renewal. It is a good time to make love potions. One way of doing this is for everyone to gather around a pot of wine or fruit juice simmering on a fire. Small bowls of spices such as cardamom, cinnamon sticks, nutmegs and allspice are offered to everyone, together with a small square of muslin. Taking a selection of spices, each person makes up their own bundle, while thinking about their wishes with regard to their sexual or creative energies. Then the bundles are offered to the pot, and everyone drinks the spicy liquid, while imagining they are imbibing what they desire.

Songs for Beltane would be old ones such as 'Greensleeves', or any love songs, the saucier the better. We may choose to continue the European custom of maypole dancing at Beltane, or find our own version of this practice, perhaps dancing around a living tree that we have decorated with ribbons and flowers. This could well be an occasion for visiting the forest, the domain of Tane, to celebrate the fertilising powers of the Maori green god, and to pay homage to one of the remaining great kauri trees. We could remember the old custom of tree clasping in both Maori and European traditions, and take time to recharge our barren energies by clasping a tree and taking in its life spirit. It may also be appropriate to reciprocate by making an offering to the trees, and asking ourselves, What can I do to help the greening of the earth at Beltane?

Beltane could become national 'green day', with people wearing a sprig of green to show that they have done something for the earth on this day – maybe writing a letter in support of tree preservation, making a donation to a conservation cause, planting a tree, or some other action. Thus 'wearing the green' becomes a sign of commitment to the earth, and Beltane becomes an opportunity to answer the call from an endangered planet. It also becomes a clear announcement to those who would dress in black, thinking it is Halloween, reminding them that this is spring, the green time in our Southern Hemisphere land.

The Beltane feast could be a green one, with salads and sprouts, new season's asparagus and kiwifruit.

Whatever we do, let this be the theme: the re-juicing of ourselves and of the earth at this spring festival.

1. Best, *Time*, p.19.

2. Best, *Time*, p. 22.

3. Simmons, p. 15.

4. Best, *Forest*, pp. 61-62, and Orbell, *Folktales*, p. 38. Raukawa leaves were also used for scent, as was speargrass and tawhiri gum which were used in sachets and the leaves strewn about in houses. Kopuru was a fragrant moss also used for scent. In the tale 'Ko Pare raua ko Hutu', Pare's house is scented with kawakawa leaves. (Orbell, *Folktales*, p. 3).

5. MacDonald, p. 49.

6. Brougham, p.68.

7. Reed, p. 225. A number of trees had this association. On Puketutu Island the Waiohua women clasped a puriri tree known as Te Pu Rakau. (Graeme Murdoch, pers. comm.) A similar custom was practised in Europe; for example in France, where women would clasp a willow tree to encourage conception: see Armstrong, p.36.

8. Best, *Astron*, p. 43.

9. Best, *Forest*, p. 82.

10. Beattie, p. 139. and Makereti pp. 203-204.

11. Best, *Forest*, pp. 87 f.

12. Beattie, p. 140.

13. Sitwell, p. 194.

14. Cooper, p. 145.

15. Sjoo, p. 34.

16. Slade, p. 85.

17. For pronunciation of Celtic names, see Rutherford, p.9.

18. Rolleston, p. 133, and Larousse, p. 244.

19. Larousse, p. 244.

20. MacCana, p. 64, and Rolleston, p. 133.

21. Matthews, p.84.

22. Matthews, pp. 91-92.

23. Stewart, p. 62.

24. Kightly, p. 159.

25. Johnson, p. 29.

26. See Ross & Robins, *The Life and Death of a Druid Prince*, for a fascinating discussion of how 'Lindow man', whose preserved body was found in an English peat bog, may have been a Beltane victim, his last meal being the charred cake found in his stomach.

27. Matthews, p. 85.

28. Sitwell, p. 364.

29. Walker, Dict, p. 253.

30. Whistler, p. 139.

31. Whistler, p. 136.

32. Barker, p. 120.

33. Anderson, p. 120.

34. Harrowven, p. 63.

35. Frazer, *Bough*, p. 159, from a Berkshire May song.

36. Frazer, *Bough*, p. 157.

37. Anderson, pp. 133-134.

38. Sachs, pp. 64-65.

39. Harrowven, p. 63.

40. Whistler, p. 149.

41. Slade, p. 98.

42. Frazer. pp. 167-171.

43. Anderson, p. 23.

44. Frazer, *Bough*, p. 173.

45. Water in streams was used for healing in the Maori tradition also (Beattie, p. 75). Pei te Hurinui Jones describes a water initiation ritual in his short story 'Te Hurinui', used to heal him of disturbing dreams (Ihimaera, p. 9). For a description of the use of sacred water among the Ngati Kahungunu to instil knowledge in new entrants to the whare wananga (the school of learning), see Mitchell, pp. 234-235. For a vivid account of his childhood initiation in a sacred pool, see Stirling, pp. 92-93, and for the use of water in tohi rituals of purification at the start of a child's life, see Hiroa, p.486.

Summer Solstice

Te Maruaroa o te Raumati

21 – 22 December

Tangi e te riroriro
Te tohu o te raumati
(Sweetly sings the grey warbler
Chant of summer days).[1]

...in summer when the coasts
bear crimson bloom, sprinkled
like blood
On the lintel of the land.
(ARD Fairburn, 'Elements')[2]

Summer solstice, the longest day, arrives as the year is coming to an end and the holiday season about to begin. Although this is when the sun's light reaches its maximum, it is but the threshold of summer. The most easily recognised sign of summer solstice in the North Island is the crimson flowering of the pohutukawa trees that fringe the coastline. Dancing against the blue sea, they announce the promise of the sunny season with its pilgrimages to the sea for swimming, fishing, water sports and simple relaxation. In the South Island it is the crimson flowers of rata that are associated with the pleasures of summer.

Aotearoa

Along the coastline and inland hills toetoe wave their feathery, yellow fronds and harakeke (flax) sticks out its nectar-filled, flame-like flowers. The small, white flowers of ngaio may still be visible. In the bush, the flowering of other plants is more hidden: scented toru on its red, hairy stalks, supplejack and kamahi in long, white, fluffy clusters, and the profuse fragrance of the tiny, white, star-like putaputaweta. Berries are swelling and ripening: karaka now shiny green, porokaiwhiri (pigeonwood) turning orange, and purple konini, the fruit of the kotukutuku, falling to the ground to be taken by rats and wild pigs. Also fruiting are red and black makomako, whose grapelike bunches of berries were eaten raw by the early Maori and picked by early Pakeha settlers to make jam or jellies. The yellow fruit of kawakawa droops from the female trees, attracting kereru (wood pigeons). Along the roadsides tanguru (olearia) waves its white, daisy-like flowers.

Titoki is now fruiting. Its juicy, red pulp was sometimes eaten by the Maori, but it was the large, shiny, black seed inside that they valued most, for this yielded oil that could be used medicinally. The seed capsules were placed into flax kits and then pounded with a club to crush them; then the bags were wrung out and the greenish-coloured oil collected. Hot stones in the kits were often used to hasten the extraction process. For extra fragrance, crushed manuka or kawakawa leaves would sometimes be added to the scented oil, which was rubbed on to the hair or body. Titoki oil was also used to make a salve or massage oil for babies or breast-feeding women to ease chafing.

Tawhaki and the pohutukawa

The pohutukawa's flowers were a vivid reminder of the god Tawhaki, who once lived on the earth as a man. One day, people cutting brushwood saw him at the top of a high hill. To their astonishment he stripped off his clothing and stood clothed in brilliant lightning: at that moment they knew he was no mere mortal. Tawhaki's cousins grew jealous of his powers and of the attention he drew from women. One day, when Tawhaki was washing and combing his hair in a pool, they set upon him, beating him viciously and leaving him for dead. He did not die however, for he healed himself with water and karakia, chanting to the red blood:

> It grows on the hair of your head,
> and on your brow the blood grows red –
> the blood, the blood of Tawhaki,
> and of the sun and moon,
> and of the auspicious sky –
> of the sky now above.[3]

Tawhaki's words greet his red blood as the very spirit of life. Its potent colour passed into the pohutukawa blossom, which became known as *te pua whero a Tawhaki* (the red flower of Tawhaki).[4]

Summer solstice marks the passing of the sixth month when 'the sun has gained strength' and 'all things greet Rangi and Papa'. It is now the seventh, known to the Tuhoe and Ngati Awa tribes as Hakihea, when *kua noho nga manu kai roto i te kohanga* ('birds are now sitting in their nests').[5] The pipiwharauroa (shining cuckoo) changes its call, to include the notes indicating plenty: 'whiti, whiti

ora', a sign that Rehua has returned and all is well. Ruatahuna children had a chant to greet the pipiwharauroa:

E manu! Tenakoe! Kua tae tenei ki te mahanatanga, kua puawai nga rakau katoa, kua pa te kakara ki te ihu o te tangata. Kua puta ano koe ki runga tioro ai, tioro i te whitu, tioro i te waru; me tioro haere ano e koe tenei kupu e whai ake ki te marae o tama ma, o hine ma. Kui! Kui! Kui! Whiti whiti ora.

(O bird! I greet you. The season of warmth has now arrived; all trees have blossomed, and their fragrance has reached the nostrils of people. Again you appear trilling on high, trilling in the seventh [month], trilling in the eighth [month]; now go forth trilling the following message at the homes of young men and women – Kui! kui! kui! Whiti whiti ora.)[6]

Rehua and Whakaonge-kai the hungry one

Summer was also announced by the appearance of the star/spirit woman Parearohi shimmering in the sky with her consort Rehua (Antares, the red star in Scorpio). Rehua had two wives: Ruhia, the enervator, and Whakaonge-kai, meaning 'she who makes food scarce', for Whakaonge-kai was always hungry. The two wives took their places, one on either side of Rehua. When he turned to Ruhia she would bring first her left foot down, and then the other foot, blessing the earth with her warmth and ripening powers. Fruit then began to swell on the trees and all creatures became languid in the heat. When Rehua turned to mate with Whakaonge-kai summer came and food was scarce, due to Whakaonge-kai's huge appetite.[7]

Rehua was sometimes also referred to as the sun and people would say karakia to Rehua: 'Rehua is the sun, and if he did not shine the grass and vegetation would die and life would cease.'[8]

Honey gathering

By now people had returned from the first cutting of the cabbage tree and went out to gather honey, known as wai korari, from flax flowers, a great delicacy in a land without honey bees.[9] Sweet things are likened to this delicious food in the saying *me te wai korari* (like the sweetness of the flax honey).[10] The nectar was said to ebb and flow in the flowers in unison with the tide; at low tide it receded, but at a spring tide it overflowed the edges of the flower.[11] In the following Ngati Porou action song the flax nectar is compared with the rushing forth of tears:

> *E te roimata ra i roto ra, ka maringi kei waho.*
> *E ai te wai korari, ka ngawha i te waru.*
> (Let the tears from within be poured forth
> Like nectar from the flax stem bursting forth in the eighth month.)[12]

Again, in a Ngati Porou lament, the nectar that flows in summer is compared with the flowing of tears:

> *He puna wai e utuhia, he wai kei aku kamo*
> *Te pua korau e ruia, e tipu i te waru.*
> (Like the springwell are tears from mine eyes
> Like the nectar shaken free, that grows in the eighth month.)[13]

The flowers would be picked at full tide and gently tapped on the sides of a gourd so the nectar would flow out. It was used for soaking and flavouring fern root, and in the South Island was mixed with para ti, the cabbage tree 'sago' (made from its roots and stems).[14] An added bonus was that the kaka was now growing fat on flax honey, and could be caught for good eating.[15]

Raupo pollen gathering

Another summer activity was the gathering of raupo pollen. In the early morning or late evening, when the pollen was moister and less likely to blow away, a large group of adults and children would go down to the swamps. After picking, they would gently shake the flowering spikes into bark vessels to collect the fine, fluffy powder. The yellow pungapunga or pua (pollen) had a light, sweetish taste and was mixed with water or gently steamed to make gingerbread-like cakes.[16]

Koreirei, the central part of the succulent, white raupo roots, was also eaten, usually raw, during the summer.[17]

Ra the sun god

It was time for the sun god, Ra, to change wives. At the takanga o te ra (changing of the sun) at the maruaroa (solstice), Ra would begin to leave his summer wife Hine-raumati, whose domain was the earth and all its food, and go to live with his winter wife, Hine-takurua, whose domain was the sea. Both were daughters of Tangaroa-akiukiu the sea god, but while the winter goddess lived with her father in the ocean, her sister was in charge of birds, forest and cultivated food products. The changeover at summer solstice seems equivalent to the European idea of the seeding of the light with the darkness to come, as the sun's power begins to decline. It also reflects a new seasonal emphasis in Maori food gathering, from land to sea.

Kaimoana (seafood)

It was now a long time since the last kumara harvest, and although the new crop was growing, the next harvest was some months away. Kaimoana, the gift of Hine-takurua, was calling.[18] The hapu (sub-tribes) that were close enough to the coast would now divide into whanau (family groups) and migrate to summer camps by the sea. There they would gather shellfish and catch fish both to eat and to dry in vast quantities in the sun for winter storage. After baking, the fish would be hung on racks or poles to dry, and later stored in pataka (food houses). If stored in an airy place, the fish would be good for three to six months. The scale of the fishing could be enormous, as in the Rarawa tribe's twice-yearly shark-school fishing in the Rangaunu Harbour in Northland. There would be elaborate preparations for the expedition shortly after summer solstice, on a January night just after full moon, and again by day two weeks later, yielding an annual catch of some 7000 sharks.[19]

The barracouta season that lasted from November to April was well under way and in the South Island canoes now went to the hapuku

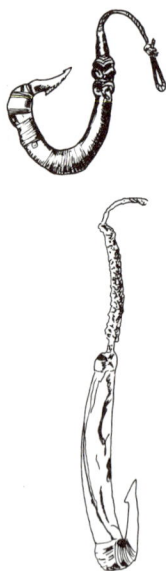

fishing grounds, bringing back great quantities of fish for the women to scale, clean, and hang on racks for drying. The hapuku season continued until winter solstice, when Orion rose and the tail of the hapuku turned red.[20] At Oruapaeroa (New Brighton Beach) in Canterbury people would both swim and catch horihori (sole) in the summer.[21]

Within living memory, we have the account by Tamati Kurupae of the summer fishing season on Lake Taupo:

> In the summer time we all went out on the lake fishing – we caught the inanga – the whitebait – in great quantities, in fine-meshed nets, and preserved it for future use, and filled our storehouses. Kokopu, too, that little fish which the trout have eaten out, like the inanga, we caught in hand-nets called pouraka. We were out in our canoes and along the shores day after day; every village was busy.[22]

Duck hunting

In the South Island the duck season began in December and continued till March, the ducks making good eating during their maunu (moulting season). Around Lake Ellesmere large numbers of putakitaki (paradise duck) were caught in fenced-off enclosures. The parera (grey duck), kukupako (black teal), tataa (brown duck) and pateke (grey teal) were also caught.[23]

Meanwhile, the old people, young women and children would stay home to look after and weed the kumara gardens. It would be an opportunity for the old to pass on teachings to the young, and to polish pounamu (greenstone). It could be a busy time, and various proverbs refer to the tendency of some to absent themselves now, only to reappear in autumn when the kumara had been harvested:

> *He huanga ki matiti, he tama ki tokerau*
> ('a distant relative in summer, a son in the autumn').[24]
> *Tu ke raumati, whakapiri ngahuru*
> ('You keep well away in summer but stick close in autumn').
> *Ha kai koutou ka hohoro, ko te ngaki e kore*
> ('You are quick to eat, but not work in the plantation').[25]

Pagan Europe

In Europe, where people knew the rigours of a hard winter, and where the sun's energy was essential to the growth of crops, summer solstice was the most popular of the fire festivals – all except for early Celtic Britain, where the greater emphasis on a pastoral tradition meant that the 'cattle-in' and 'cattle out' times of Samhain and Beltane were more significant. In the old Celtic Coligny calendar summer solstice marked the transition between the 'time of brightness' and 'horse time', when people went visiting.[28]

Solstice means 'sun stand still', and this is exactly what it appeared to do over the days of its turning. People used hills, trees or stones as markers to discover the crucial moment. In ancient stone sites, the solstice sun magically illuminated symbols inscribed on rocks.

Solstice later became known as midsummer's day and from Ireland to Russia, Scandinavia to the Mediterranean, either the day or eve of midsummer was celebrated with fire rituals. So tenacious are the old pagan customs that even in Morocco and Algiers people still light bonfires at summer solstice, despite the fact that in Muslim society the official lunar calendar does not recognise sun festivals.[29]

As with winter solstice, it took three or four days before observers could be sure that the sun had 'turned' and so the main celebrations were on 24 June rather than the 21st or 22nd.

Summer solstice came when the agricultural cycle demanded hard work. Sheep were shorn now, or a little earlier, the fields had to be weeded and hoed, and hay-making meant that all hands were called on to help. In some districts people went out to the bogs to cut peat, dry it in the sun and bring it back to the villages for storing as fuel.

Whereas winter solstice was a festival of hope, being a celebration of the sun's birth, summer solstice was a more complex time. On the one hand, it was a season of fullness and ripening; on the other hand it signalled apprehension. From this moment the sun's energy would begin to decline; time was running out; the full-blown rose would soon drop its petals and die. At winter solstice people let themselves go in riotous feasting and revelry, knowing that one thing was certain: the darkest night was now safely behind them. Summer solstice was no such time for irresponsible festivities, for people had to look ahead and plan for the darkening season. Whether bringing in the hay while anxiously watching the sky for rain, or bringing in the peat, they knew the necessity of storing the sun's energies in time for winter. Their summer solstice rituals focused on sympathetic magic to entice the sun to stay.

Solstice fires

Three main features characterised the celebrations. Most important were the bonfires, lit in villages and on hilltops all over Europe in a spectacular homage to the sun's power. European peasants believed that the corn would ripen for as far as the bonfire light was visible; even if they could not stop the sun, at least they could kindle an earthly sun that would magically quicken the growth of their vital crops.[30] The fires would often be kindled at midnight, and it was common for young men and women to stay up all night, dancing in the light of the fires, tossing flowers and herbs into the flames.

Often the very act of kindling the fire was significant, being done through the friction of oak (male) and fir (female) wood. In some areas such as Cumbria the magical rowan wood was used in the fire. In Cornwall, where bonfire lighting was revived in 1929, a flower-decked woman symbolising the Earth Goddess and known as the Lady of the Flowers, throws her bouquet of flowers and herbs on to the wood before it is lit, as a symbolic sacrifice.[31] In older times the sacrifice was more likely to have been a human one, later replaced with an effigy. Summer solstice was time to gather many herbs, such as rue, vervain, lavender, woodbine and the sun-yellow St John's wort, which would be worn as purification or thrown into the fire to burn away bad luck. As an example of the scope of the solstice recognition, in 16th-century Germany almost every village had a public fire which people would look at through bunches of larkspur held in their hands in order to keep their eyes healthy for the coming year – no doubt a practical measure if the fire was a bright one, besides serving as a spell. Before they left, they threw mugwort and vervain into the fire to burn away bad luck,[32] vervain being a purifying herb whose properties were also known by the Druids. In Britain, violets and verbena were other plants offered to the solstice bonfires.[33]

In some parts of Europe people with special powers, such as the priestesses of Artemis, took part in fire-walking, crossing a path of burning coals with bare feet to test themselves against the full power of the sun.[34]

Solstice processions

A second important activity was the procession around the fields with flaming torches to invoke growth for the crops, no doubt another attempt to keep the sun's energy available for as long as possible. Often the bonfire ash would be brought to the fields to add fertilising power.

Solstice fire wheels

A third feature was the fire wheels. An old cart-wheel would be bound with straw, set ablaze from the solstice bonfire, and sent rolling down the hill. The sight of this fiery wheel, madly bouncing downwards in the midnight darkness, must have stirred unease in the minds of those who watched and ran with it, even as they cheered it on. For sooner or later it would come to rest and the blaze would die. Consciously or unconsciously, the watchers would know they had just witnessed the descent of the sun from its height in the heavens.[35]

Fern seed

Midsummer was also a gathering time, for the solemn rite of cutting mistletoe from the oak groves with a golden sickle, and in a lighter vein, the gathering of 'fern seed'. This was actually the tiny spores on the underside of fern leaves, which were gathered at midnight and put inside one shoe to make the wearer as invisible as the 'fern seed' itself.[36]

Water rituals

There were also midsummer water rituals throughout the ancient world. In Babylon and Carthage people bathed an image of the god Tammuz, whose name meant 'true son of deep water'. Sacred rivers, wells and the sea were said to take on healing powers on Midsummer's Eve and many people either bathed in these waters, or washed themselves in the morning dew.

Christian Europe: St John's Day

The Church banned midsummer bonfires, finding their paganism disturbing, but the water symbolism was taken up and linked with baptism. According to St Luke's Gospel 24 June was the birth day of St John the Baptist, and so the summer solstice rituals were superseded by the rites of St John's Day. The leaders of the early Church even took the old invocations to Bel, the Celtic god of light, and dedicated them to St John. But the old customs lived on. People persisted in lighting bonfires on hills at midsummer, and leaping through the flames for good luck.

Medieval festivities

Throughout medieval times midsummer was celebrated, with everyone circling a bonfire clockwise, the direction of the sun. Each person wore a birch-wreath crown, or a sprig of new green leaves over the heart. As they circled the fire, they carried candles and chanted the midsummer riddle:

> Green is Gold
> Fire is Wet
> Future's Told
> Dragon's Net.

Each line contained a hidden question, with answers as follows: When is green gold? – at midsummer, because the new leaves have a bronze or gold appearance. How can fire be wet? – because it was the custom to float small candles on water as a way of making a wish for the future. If the small candle boat reached the other side of the pond, the wish would come true. 'Future's told' referred to the fact that midsummer was the time for divining the future, especially for young people who wished to marry. 'Dragon's net' referred to the requirement that each reveller should 'kill a dragon', usually in the symbolic form of a pastry or maybe a dragon kite.

Divining the future took place by breaking a raw egg into a small bowl and reading prophesies into the shape it formed, or by plucking the petals of the midsummer rose to discover whether s/he loves me or loves me not. Destiny cakes were made in different shapes and chosen from under a cloth, a forerunner of the 'fortune cookies' that are still made today. A leafy branch of St John's wort was given to each guest, and its state of freshness at the end of the feast or the next morning revealed, whether for them, love would be durable or not.

Food and drink

St John's bread was eaten at the feast. It was not really bread, but the seed of the locust tree, better known today as carob. It was supposed to have sustained St John when he went into the desert. The feasting drink was cuckoo-foot ale, in honour of the bird that arrived in spring and brought in the summer. The cuckoo was noticed to change its song at midsummer and to begin to sing 'cuck-cuckoo' instead of just 'cuckoo', very like the way the pipiwharauroa was observed by the Maori to add to its song from spring to summer. Old country rhymes referred to this, and the various stages of the cuckoo's visit:

In April Cuckoo sings his lay
In May I sing all day.
In June I change my tune,
In July away I fly
In August go I must.

And

The cuckoo is a fine bird,
She whistles as she flies
And as she whistles, Cuckoo!
The bluer grow the skies.[37]

Songs and poems told of the cuckoo's call:

Summer is a-coming in
Loudly sing, cuckoo!
The seed grows
The meadow blows
And the woods spring anew.
Sing, cuckoo!
Cuckoo! Cuckoo!
Well do you sing, cuckoo!
Never cease singing now.

The celebration ended with another circuit of the bonfire by people holding candles and once more chanting the riddle seven times. Finally they would do the processional dance of 'threading the needle', in order to sew the traditions into the fabric of life.[38]

Rituals for today

Summer solstice represents a lost opportunity. We have imported Christmas, rooted in the winter solstice celebrations of Yule, into our Southern Hemisphere calendar. Here it falls in summer, just after the longest day, and the result is a clashing of symbols. In summer sunshine many of us still enact the customs of a winter festival, cooking hot dinners with turkey and roast vegetables, mince pies and plum pudding until we become totally inert. To make matters worse, we now break from the working year to take our summer holidays. The result is confusion, tension and stress. Many of us hate Christmas.

It would be far better to let go of all pretence, and to relax and

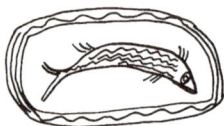

accept this time as a summer festival. The Church made a conscious decision to identify the birth of Christ with the old rituals around the birth of the sun on the darkest night; likewise we could free ourselves enormously were we to shift Christmas to its natural place at winter solstice, and celebrate the height of summer in its own right.

In both Maori and European traditions summer solstice was a time of hard work, whether in the fields with shearing or haymaking, hoeing and weeding the crops, or catching and drying fish. The sun was as essential for the drying of fish and hay as for the ripening of grain or kumara crops.

Today, summer solstice still falls at a time of hard work, as we wind up the year, but this time it precedes a season of relaxation and holiday for most people. So how do we bring all these elements together into solstice rituals for today?

First, we might take time to meet with friends, and focus our attention on the sun. Children could be encouraged to draw sun pictures. Everyone might bring a sun symbol to hang on a tree outside: an orange tree would be ideal. Summer solstice plants could be used for decorations: the red blossoms of our solstice tree, the pohutukawa, te pua whero a Tawhaki (the red flower of Tawhaki), or the flame-like heads of toetoe and harakeke (flax). Roses may be included, the rose being a symbol of the full blooming of the solstice.

It is time to honour Mahuika, the Maori fire goddess who held this power in her flaming fingernails until Maui came to steal it. In the European tradition this is the time of the Goddess as Woman, pregnant with new life, and of the crowning of the Corn King: relationship in its fullness. It is a good time for weddings.

We can look into the sky to see Rehua, the summer star. The movement of Ra out to sea to dwell with Hine-takurua, the winter goddess and guardian of kaimoana, may be ritually marked by moving an image of the sun from a place amongst green leaves to a place amongst sea shells, and taking time to contemplate the meaning of this shift. In our rituals we remember that this is the turning of the sun and the darkness is now seeded.

Summer solstice is a good time to tell the story of how Maui tried to steal the sun. Just as the people of Europe wanted to make the sun

stay longer, and used fire magic to encourage this to happen, so did Maui want to get more sun power. The sun god crossed the sky each day too fast for Maui's liking, so together with his brothers, Maui went to the great pit where the sun god slept each night. There they lay in wait with strong flax ropes. When morning came and the sun god rose out of the pit Maui and his brothers threw the ropes, snaring the sun. An enormous struggle ensued, with the sun god thrashing from side to side to get free. Eventually he crawled out, still alive but greatly disabled, and from that time he moved slowly across the sky, no longer able to go with speed. He also emerged from the struggle having lost something more precious, for inadvertently he revealed his secret name, Tama-nui-te-ra, meaning Great Son of the Day, and by doing so, lost some of his power.

For a family summer solstice ritual held by my ritual group a few years ago the father of some of the children dressed in yellow with a high crown as the Sun King, and emerged from the bottom of the garden after everyone had enticed him out by ringing bells and cymbals. He brought with him a basket of gifts and gave them out to each person in turn.

For a solstice ritual, each person could bring a symbol of the sun, or of what they are manifesting at this season. Together we may acknowledge the moment of greatest light, the zenith of our own energies and our achievements of the year. We may honour the achievements of others as well, seeing the sun in one another. It is a time of positivity and affirmation, and one way to do this is to give a gift of recognition to our friends and family members. We could send a card or letter, affirming them for their achievements over the year or giving thanks for help we have received. Summer solstice is the ideal time to give out our radiance to others. Another way of doing this would be to give a red flower, a rose or pohutukawa perhaps, to someone we care for, as a sign of affection.

As we give and receive this bounty we allow ourselves to become conscious of the fullness that is needed for whatever lean times lie ahead.

It could be a time to link with family and friends in a simple way, knowing that the big gatherings are to be kept until winter solstice. Or

if we did feel more expansive, we might hold community carnivals with dancing in the streets and firework displays.

Food for summer solstice could take the form of a sun feast, with the colours red, orange and yellow being keynotes: have fun putting together beetroot and carrots, new season's tomatoes and yellow courgettes or capsicums, with sun fruits to follow: strawberries, bananas, oranges, tangelos, and pineapples. In Aotearoa this was the season for fish and ducks, so maybe seafood, duck or chicken would feature in the sun feast. To be really traditional, we might add small dishes of raupo pollen, or even make pollen cakes, and add some harakeke (flax) nectar or a dish of honey. The solstice cake could be a honey cake, round and yellow as the sun, and studded with sunflower seeds.

For most people, summer solstice is the threshold to the holiday season, and by giving thanks for what has been completed, we can let go of the working year and step forward and enjoy the break that lies ahead.

1. For the full greeting chant to the riroriro, herald of summer, see Pomare, p. 293.

2. Curnow, ed, p. 150.

3. Alpers, pp. 106-108.

4. Best, *Astron*, pp. 8-9.

5. Best, *Time*, p. 19.

6. Best, *Forest*, p. 339.

7. Best, *Astron*, p. 57, and *Time*, p. 26.

8. Beattie, p. 43, quoting Tikao.

9. Best, *Forest*, p. 83 and p.100. Although there were, and still are, native bees, they are solitary, living in tunnels and clay banks. The introduced honey bees, on the other hand, are social bees that operate in swarms. Their specialised social structure allows for efficient and widespread nectar gathering carried out by the worker. An old Maori informant told Elsdon Best in 1874 that the introduction of the social honey bees, along with cats and rats, was responsible for a decline in the numbers of nectar-eating native birds: 'the bee is especially harmful. The disappearance of the hordes of birds from our forests has a depressing effect on us.' (Best, *Forest*, p. 115).

10. Brougham, p. 114.

11. Best, *Forest*, p. 100.

12. Ngata, *Nga Moteatea II*, pp. 26-27.

13. Ngata, *Nga Moteatea II*, pp. 120-121.

14. Best, *Forest*, p. 100.

15. Best, *Forest*, p. 199.

16. Orbell, *Nat. World*, p. 43 and Best, *Forest*, p. 68.

17. Makereti, p. 213, and Beattie, p. 139.

18. Best, *Astron*, p. 18.

19. Orbell, pp. 30-31.

20. Best, *Fish*, pp. 53-54.

21. Beattie, p. 136.

22. Pomare, p. 179.

23. Beattie, p. 133.

24. Brougham, pp. 79-80.

25. Brougham, p. 65.

26. Sitwell, p. 392.

27. Hayward, ed, p. 293.

28. Matthews, p. 92.

29. Frazer, *Bough*, pp.827-828.

30. Frazer, *Bough*, p. 845.

31. Durdin-Robertson, p. 125.

32. Frazer, *Bough*, p. 815.

33. Whistler, p. 167.

34. Cooper, p. 93.

35. Frazer, *Bough*, p. 816, and Cooper, p. 92.

36. Campanelli, pp. 84-86.

37. Holden, p. 86.

38. Cosman, pp. 57-60.

First Fruits/
Lean Time

Te Waru, Lugnasad, Lammas

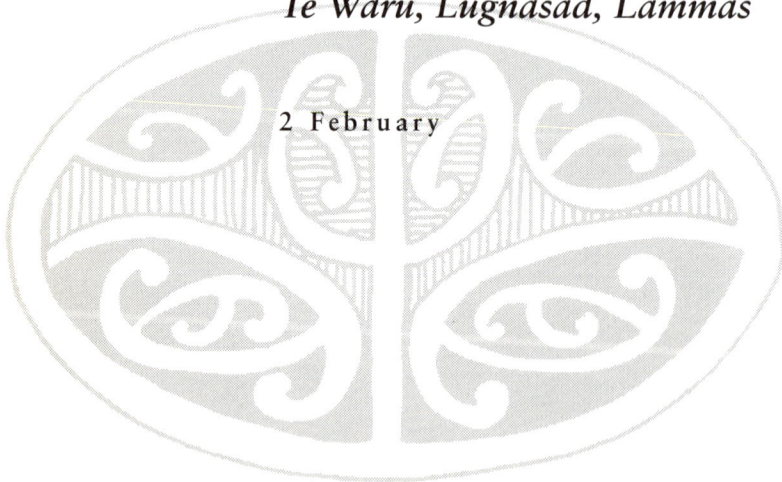

2 February

First Fruits lies half-way between summer solstice and autumn equinox. Although the days are now perceptibly growing shorter, the weather is still hot and dry and it may feel as if summer could last forever. The flowering of summer solstice has passed into the fruiting season. While late-flowering trees such as rata and snow-white cascades of houhere (lacebark) may be beginning their spectacular displays, most of the native trees are now fruiting: the tall kahikatea, matai, kawakawa, totara, and large ti (cabbage tree) with its clusters of small, bluish-white berries. Orange karaka berries stand out brightly against dark green leaves, as referred to in the Maori song line te *karaka whakaura i te waru* ('karaka reddening in the eighth month').[3] Taraire is in fruit and kereru flock to feed on tawa berries, while tawhiwhi and lancewood join the late-flowering trees.

Aotearoa

In the old Maori calendar this was kohitatea, the eighth lunar month, when *kua makura te kai; ka kai te tangata i nga kai hou o te tau* ('fruits have now set and people eat the first fruits of the year'). It was also said: *ka kauawhi a Papa i nga mokopuna i konei* ('now Papa embraces her grandchildren').[4] Young gourds might now be ready to eat, but the kumara still had much growing to do. It was the month when the long-tailed and shining cuckoos koekoea and pipiwharauroa began to leave for the north. Cicadas sang loudly, as referred to in the proverb *Me te tarakihi e papa ana i te waru* ('like cicadas chattering in the eighth month').[5]

Other proverbs referred to this season: *He puanga kakaho, ke rere i te waru* ('the bloom of the toetoe flies in the eighth'),[6] and *Tukua atu*

Nga ra o te waru e
(The days of the eighth month when food is scarce)[1]

The rata blooms explode
(James K Baxter, *Autumn Testament*)[2]

ki tua, ki nga ra o te waru e ('leave it for the future, for the days when food is scarce'), the eighth month being a colloquial expression for the lean time preceding harvest.[7] Fungi were observed to flourish during a *tau hi roki*, or lean season, and would be gathered now if other supplies were short.[8] The lean season is referred to in a saying about how important it was for a man's daughter to marry a good provider: *Mau, ma te mangere taku tamaiti, ma te tangata ra i te pupu paka taku tamaiti, kia taea ai te riri nga ra roroa o te waru* ('is my child to be for an indolent person like you? no, my child is for the industrious man, he who has a full food store, so that she may combat the long days of the eighth month').[9]

In some districts titoki fruit ripened now, and was linked with the blossoming of the red rata: as the proverb says, *Taute te titoki, whero te rata i te waru* ('the titoki ripens its fruit; the rata is red in the eighth month').[10] The profuse flowering of rata attracted tui and kaka. Rata nectar was known as wai kaihua and the rata feasting time that began in January, rarangi tahi. As the proverb says, *Ka kai te kaka i te wai kaihua, ka kia he rarangi tahi* ('when the kaka eat the honey of the rata flower, then the birds will be plentiful').[11] The flowering of the rata made possible a summer fowling season, for kaka and tui were now both plentiful and good to eat again, to the extent that they could be directly speared as well as being taken with snares.

In the South Island the kakapo went to the plains in search of ripe tutu berries, and were hunted on clear moonlit nights with the help of sticks and the small, fox-like kuri (dog).[12] At Rotomahana in the North Island, the Tuhourangi people hunted parera (ducks) in February, also with the help of dogs.[13] In the South Island the duck-hunting season was in full swing.

Fishing

The taking of young eels was now coming to an end. They would be caught in fern fronds as they attempted to ascend rocky parts of rivers, or caught in nets. Mud eels would now be coming into season. The dry part of summer when rivers were low was time for the repairing and building of large eel weirs, made out of manuka, matai and kareao (supplejack) ready for the following season. If the river was tidal, this work could be done at low tide.[14]

Stars

Rehua (Antares) was the summer star, personifying heat and the power to ripen all fruits, the star that governed the migration of whitebait,[15] with many proverbs indicating its importance or that of his wife Ruhia. Ruhi means 'languid' or 'enervated' in vernacular speech, and her full name of Ruhi-te-rangi was used by some tribes for the ninth month spanning February and March.[16] Ruhi may be seen in the sky as a small star near Rehua (Antares).

Kaore ana a Rehua i tatu ki raro ('Rehua has not yet alighted') referred to the stage before fruit has formed on the trees, and *Kua tatu nga waewae o Rehua kei raro* ('the feet of Rehua have rested below') referred to a hot day, when people's energy was sapped.[17] Similarly, the saying *Ko Rehua whakaruhi tangata* ('Rehua weakens humankind') revealed the effect of this star. On a hot day people would say *Kua tahu a Rehua* ('Rehua has burnt/kindled').[18] Other proverbs refer to te paki o Ruhia ('the fine weather of Ruhia') and the heat that she brings.

On a more sinister note was the saying *Rehua kai tangata* ('people become food for Rehua'), for now that the planting season was over men were again free for raiding expeditions.[19] Food was scarce now, and the proverb *Ko Rehua pona nui* (Rehua the big jointed), refers to the fact that summer food shortages could leave people thin, with their joints protruding.[20]

Matiti, the star whose name also means summer (although raumati is the more common name), continues to be visible. There were five divisions of Matiti: Matiti-tau, beginning in November, then Matiti-hana, Matiti-kaiwai, Matiti-kaipaenga, and finally Matiti-ruwai in April.[21] First Fruits would have preceded Matiti-kaipaenga, the 'food threshold' that led forward into the harvest. Uruao, the tail of Scorpio, can now also be seen. It was said, *Ko Matiti ki te ao, ko Uruao ki runga* ('when Matiti is to be seen, Uruao is above').[22]

Harvesting ti para

It was the season for people to return to the bush or plantations for the second cutting of ti para, the cabbage tree. The first cutting was now dry and would be carried home by a big working party. They felled the metre-high young trees and stripped away the spongy outer part in order to reach the sugary core; pieces cut from it would be put out to dry and then stored in the food-houses. In winter when food was short the pieces could be soaked in water to soften them before eating. Ti para was a valued food, a 'gluey mass' with a sweet taste, used on long journeys in times of war.[23] The tap roots and tender shoots of the cabbage tree were also eaten.

Kumara pits

The kumara food pits would be prepared now, ready for the impending harvest. They were a sophisticated and successful means of storage, and a key to the survival of the Maori when they established themselves in Aotearoa, adapting to a cooler land. Kumara would not grow all year round here as it had done back in the islands of Polynesia, so pits were excavated into slopes or hillsides, or on well-drained ridges, with a small opening made. The floor was covered with gravel after the pits had been lined with kaponga, i.e. slabs of mamaku (tree fern), which not only provided a hard surface but also had a smell that kept away rats. Bracken, manuka brush and fern leaves were then laid down to soften the floor and the rua kumara (kumara pits) were now ready to receive the crop.[24]

Bush clearing

Where new ground was being cleared from the bush for future gardens it was time to attend to the large trees that in winter had been scarfed, felled and left to dry in the sun. By now they had dried out enough to be readily burnt and left to lie again until the fourth month of the following year, when the burnt pieces were cut small and worked into the soil to fertilise it for spring planting.[25]

Weeding

In the plantations women continued weeding and the workers burned green branches of kawakawa between the kumara rows in order to kill off the caterpillar pests.

Berry harvest

Many of the edible berries were now ripening on the trees. The men gathered black matai berries by climbing high in the trees with baskets or shaking the fruit on to mats spread out on the ground under laden branches. Kawakawa fruit was picked and could be eaten raw, as long as its small black seeds were spat out, or it was used to flavour a jelly made from seaweed. Makomako, the wineberry, was also eaten raw, or squeezed to make a thick, sweetish drink.[26] Available too were the bitter, tiny, dark purple kapuka (papauma) berries if food was short, and the sweet, large, purple fruit of the kotukutuku, known as konini. These were collected by the same method as that used for miro; they were good to eat, and especially enjoyed by children.

Purple hinau berries, about the size of a small damson plum, were gathered in large quantities for their flesh. After soaking in a wooden trough they were rubbed between the hands or crushed in a ngehinge-hi, a kind of tourniquet made of plaited supplejack vine. A creaking sound was emitted during this process, a sound so distinctive as to become the basis of a saying used to encourage a harsh singer to tone down their voice: *Kia ata whakawiri i te ngehingehi* ('don't twist the tourniquet').[27] The hinau skin and nut were strained and the water drained off; then the coarse meal that remained was made into a large cake and cooked for several hours in a hangi, resulting in a food that was considered a great luxury.[28]

Tutu berries were valued for their juice, although care had to be taken not to eat the highly poisonous black seeds. As with flax nectar, the juice was said to ebb and flow with the tide, and so gathering would take place at full tide. Huge quantities of berries would be harvested and squeezed in plaited, tapered bags, the juice being collected out of the funnel at the bottom. The resulting thick, deep purple juice was known as wai puhou and made a refreshing sweet summer drink.[29]

It would be left in gourds to evaporate, or allowed to ferment, then sea-weed or fern root could be soaked in it for flavouring. The juice was also made into a jelly with kelp and known as rehia.[30]

Ripe tawa berries, known as pokerehu or ponguru, could also be eaten raw, but were rather astringent. It was said that the kereru got its hoarse voice from eating tawa berries, and could no longer sing loud-ly like other birds.[31] When roasted on a fire, which would then be called ahi tawa, the berries burst open with a loud bang; hence the say-ing about chattering children: *Ko te ahi tawa hai whakarite* ('they are as noisy as a tawa fire'). Another saying likens the noise to that of a tarakihi fish in the ocean: *He ahi tawa ki uta, he kumu tarakihi ki te moana* ('a tawa fire on land and a tarakihi fish at sea').[32] The pulp of the tawa berry yielded readily, and gave rise to a metaphor for a cow-ard in the proverb *He tawa para, he whati kau tana* ('the pulp of the tawa berry is easily crushed'). On the other hand, the tawa kernel was hard, like a fierce warrior: *Ka mahi te tawa uho ki te riri* ('well done, hard kernel, fighting away!')[33] Special treatment was needed to soften the highly prized kernels: the berries were steamed for two days in a hangi, after which time the kernels could be sun-dried and kept for years. They were very hard and similar to dates.[34]

The large, dark purple taraire fruit was also steamed for two days and eaten as a staple food. The orange berries of the karaka required more complex treatment in order to transform them from a highly poi-sonous fruit to one that was extremely edible; after several days cook-ing in the hangi, they were soaked for weeks in a running stream.[35] Anyone eating karaka berries cooked like ordinary food without this special treatment risked dying from convulsions: as the proverb says, *Ki te kainga werata te karaka ka roria* ('if karaka kernels are eaten hot, the body will be distorted').[36]

Te waru, being a lean time, was not appropriate for receiving visi-tors; that would be left until harvest. As the proverb says, *Kauaka i te wa o te waru, engari hei te ngahuru* ('not to be at the time of the eighth [month], but at the harvest').[37]

Pagan Europe

In Europe, First Fruits was known as Lugnasad and took place on 2 August. As in Maori society it was a traditional time to gather berries, especially bilberries, but most important of all, it was harvest time. Corn,[39] the staple crop of Europe, was ready for harvest. Rituals marked the sacrificial death of the Grain God, who was now yielded up to the Great Goddess. The dark womb that claimed him was evoked at sacred mounds going back to neolithic times. At Silbury Hill important rites took place at harvest. The Goddess herself underwent transformation; having reached fruition, it was time for her to go underground to be slowly transformed into her Crone/Hecate/Cailleach aspect and emerge as such at Samhain.

Celtic Lugnasad

In the Celtic Coligny calendar, this was 'claim time', when tribes gathered for Lugnasad festivals and harvest fairs. Nasad meant a tribal assembly for fairs or games. Lugnasad, the harvest festival, honoured the grain god Lugh (pronounced Lookh) who died with the reaping of the crop. He was sacrificed to the Earth Goddess or Harvest Mother, who took him back into her body so that new life might emerge in the spring. The festivals of Lugnasad celebrated both Lugh and the Earth Goddess, for the two were in close association.

In Ireland the feast of Lugnasad was held in honour of the goddess of sovereignty, who had several forms. As Tailtiu she was the foster-mother of Lugh and died of exhaustion after clearing the lands of Ireland for cultivation. From this time Lugh held a festival for her in commemoration. Similarly the death of the Magda, exhausted after a great feat, was commemorated annually, as was that of the goddess Carman. These goddesses were associated with the cultivation of Ireland and its fertility.[40] Although crop-raising was not a major feature of the Celtic economy in Britain, primitive corn-growing took place in Ireland as early as neolithic times.[41]

The year growing ancient,
Not yet on summer's death,
nor on the birth
Of trembling winter…
(Shakespeare, *A Winter's Tale*)

To bend with apples the
moss'd cottage trees,
And fill all fruit with ripeness
to the core;
To swell the gourd, and
plump the hazel shells
With a sweet kernel; to set
budding more,
And still more, late flowers
for the bees,
Until they think warm days
will never cease.
(Keats, *To Autumn*)[38]

Lugh the shining one

Lugh himself was son of the Dagda, the god of life, and his name meant 'light' or 'shining'. In Irish legends he represents the triumph of light over darkness and was known as Lugh Lamhflada ('Lugh of the long arm'), referring to his magical spear and sling that gave him the power to slay enemies at long distance. The destructive power of his legendary spear was said to be so great that it could set a town alight – unless its head were kept immersed in a cauldron. This tells all: the phallic/lightning power of the masculine needs to be contained by the feminine power. Even though Lugh's name may mean 'light' and he is the hero who conquers darkness, he must submit to the greater power of the seasonal round, the cycle of the Great Goddess herself. At Lugnasad he dies with the reaping of the grain and enters the dark womb of the mother, to be reborn in spring.

Both his dying and his heroic qualities were commemorated at Lugnasad. He was sam ildanach, the master of all skills: a metal crafts-man, smith, wright, champion, harper, hero, poet, historian, and cup-bearer, very like the god Mercury who was also patron of arts and crafts. Lugh was the noble warrior in the Irish sagas who wore a green cloak, silk shirt and golden sandals. Ravens flew about his head and perched on his shoulders, giving him information.[42] Many of Lugh's qualities lived on in the form of King Arthur's knight, Lancelot.

At his festival many sports and tests of skill were held, and many of the centres for the harvest games were towns that still bear his name: Lyons in France, which was the capital of Gaul, Leiden in Holland and Carlisle in the north of England, all names derived from Lugodunum, meaning 'the town or enclosure of Lugh'. It is believed also to be the origin of the name of London, where Lugh's Gate (now Ludgate) was the site of his sacrifice and entry into the underworld, passing a great stone called Crom Curuaich.

Welsh Llew

In Wales Lugh was known as Llew and associated with the Goddess through his Lugnasad marriage to the maiden Blodeuwedd (pronounced Blod-*ai*-weth), the beautiful flower goddess who was magically formed out of blossoms. Her name literally meant 'flower-face'. A bonfire would be made on a high hill top at Lugnasad, and a heavy oak wagon wheel heated in it. When the wheel was glowing red it would be bowled downhill while the whole community watched, looking for omens in the way it went. It was another version of the ritual, held elsewhere at midsummer, that symbolised the descent of the sun from its summer height.

At Tailten, the old sacred goddess site in Ireland, the rites of Lugnasad survived into Christian times. Tailtiu became a notorious place of promiscuity due to one of the festival games of contracting an informal 'marriage' at Lugnasad, to last a year and a day. The term 'Tailten marriage' lived on, referring to a casual love affair.

Christian Europe: Lammas

The Church took over Lugnasad as the festival of Lammas, assigning it to the commemoration of St Peter's imprisonment.[44] However, the old Lugnasad continued to resonate. In Ireland, Armagh the city of the goddess Macha, who was important to Lugnasad, became the centre for Celtic Christianity. This was part of a pattern already mentioned where the early missionaries chose places already charged with spiritual power from which to do their work.[45]

The attempted linking with St Peter never really took hold, and the Church in its harvest festival of Lammas took on some of the old customs of Lugnasad. It was common for loaves made from the first corn to be brought to the church for blessings, just as they had once been offered to the Goddess. The resonance of harvest with the old earth-connected ways was too strong to ignore. Throughout the Middle Ages the corn goddesses continued to be worshipped in secret rites despite efforts by the Church to stamp out the old customs.

Lammas was very much an Anglo-Saxon occasion, the word itself coming from Saxon hlaf-mass, meaning loaf-mass or bread-feast. It was a major festival all over Europe, with various goddesses presiding

We have ploughed,
we have sowed,
We have reaped,
we have mowed,
We have brought home
every load,
Hip, hip, hip, Harvest Home!
(English harvest song)[43]

over the ripening harvest: Ops, Ceres (whose name is reflected in the word cereal), Demeter, and Juno Augusta, whose sacred month this was. At Eleusis in Greece offerings of the first barley or wheat were made to Demeter and huge granaries were built to store the grain.[46] It was considered an auspicious month in which to be born or to give birth, for the Lammas moon shone with favour on both the harvest and new babies.

Ireland retained its strong pagan links with the land. At the rite of Lammas Towers, people danced around an effigy of the Harvest Mother. The pastoral tradition was reflected in the concept of Lammas land, which was private property until Lammas Day when it became subject to the common rights of pasturage until spring.

Fertility customs

Other customs carried on the old fertility associations. Many fairs were held for the selling of the newly fat lambs. At Lammas Fair at Kirkwall in the Orkneys, young men and women picked Lammas 'brothers' and 'sisters', to be their lovers for the duration of the festival. They set out rows of sheaves in a 'long bed' on the barn floor, and after the young women had spent the evening carding wool, they would be joined on the long beds by the young men.[47] On the Isle of Man people climbed to the top of mountains and hills. One peak called Snaefell became notorious for the 'rude and indecent' behaviour of the people who climbed it at Lammas.[48]

The Lammas tree

The Lammas tree was a hazel, ruled by Mercury and known as Coll by the Celts. The association reflects the old magic, for its forked twigs were used for water divining and the term 'witch hazel' points to its connection with the goddess. In Britain hazel-nuts were studied to make predictions about the coming weather:

If the nutshells are thick, winter will be bleak.
If the nutshells are thin, winter will be mild.

Rituals for today

In both European and Maori traditions this was the berry time, and at the simplest level the First Fruits ritual of 2 February might be a berry feast of all the seasonal berries, sweetened with rata honey. The table could be graced with the blossom of rata and houhere. The leaving of the pipiwharauroa and koekoea would be noted as a sign of the advancing of the year and the declining light. With them the holiday season for many is left behind, for school and other institutions of learning now begin again.

It is also possible to follow the European traditions of Lugnasad and Lammas, by celebrating with homemade bread or the first ears of sweet corn. The theme of this season is the ageing of the year as the Corn Mother becomes the Crone and the warrior Sun King Lugh is soon to be felled.

There is also an opportunity to go further. At this season we are faced with divergent meanings, depending on which cultural tradition we look at. In the European grain cycle of wheat and barley, it is the beginning of harvest, and the first loaves of bread are offered to the Great Mother. In the Maori cycle of the kumara, it is not yet harvest; in fact far from being a time of plenty it is te waru patote, the lean month,[49] when the staple crop is at its scarcest.

So how might we celebrate First Fruits or Te Waru today? Do we make harvest rituals or do we mark the lean time? The answer is both. We can allow the discrepancy to speak to us. While the European ovens are full, the Maori rua (storage pits) are empty. It is not harvest for everyone in our land; economic discrepancies are a reality. As the poet Henare Dewes has so eloquently written:

> My people cry out
> But the baskets of food are empty
> And the promises that filled them,
> nurture the thistles
> of abandoned courtyards.[50]

Our rituals could consciously reflect this reality, using dual sets of symbols in contrast with each other:

the loaf of bread	the empty kete (kit)
ears of sweet corn	a handful of native berries such as karaka or tutu
stalks of wheat	fronds of toetoe.

Let this be the Festival of the Half Harvest, a time to reflect on inequalities of wealth distribution and to consider how resources may be shared. We could make an altar or centre-piece divided down the middle, with symbols of plenty on one side, and symbols of scarcity on the other. Moving something such as bread (whether actual or in its colloquial meaning of money) from one side to the other would be a symbolic enactment of resource-sharing. We could then make this intention a reality by committing ourselves to some action. This could be the season of pledges and koha, for generous giving of our own harvest, whether inner or outer.

1. Brougham, p.91.

2. Baxter, p. 34.

3. Best, *Forest*, p.129.

4. Best, *Time*, p. 19 and p. 22.

5. Brougham. p. 114.

6. Brougham, p. 81.

7. Brougham, p. 91.

8. Best, *Forest*, p. 99.

9. Best, *Forest*, p. 84.

10. Brougham, p. 70.

11. Brougham, p. 57, and Best, *Forest*, pp. 198-199.

12. Best, *Forest*, p. 173.

13. Makereti, p. 267.

14. Makereti, pp. 245-246.

15. Best, *Astron*, p. 57.

16. Best, *Time*, pp. 19-20.

17. Brougham, p. 113.

18. Best, *Astron*, p. 56.

19. Brougham, p. 113.

20. Best, *Astron*, p. 56.

21. Best, *Astron*, p. 55.

22. Simmons, p. 17.

23. Makereti, p. 211.

24. Makereti, pp. 195-196.

25. Simmons, p. 13.

26. Makereti, p. 212.

27. Brougham, p. 124.

28. Makereti, p. 211 and Beattie, p. 139.

29. Makereti, p. 210.

30. Beattie, p. 139.

31. Riley, 41-1.

32. Best, *Forest*, p.42.

33. Brougham, p. 19. See also Riley, 2-8: *He riri ano ta te tawa uho, he riri ano ta te tawa para* ('the strength of the tawa kernel is greater than that of the surrounding flesh').

34. Makereti, pp. 206 -207.

35. Tikao says they would be steamed for 24 hours or soaked for months in water, and when dried they were known as 'Maori nuts'; also that the karaka was brought to Kaikoura by the Kai Tahu (Beattie, p. 139).

36. Riley, 70-6.

37. Mitchell, p. 264 (Ngati Kahungunu).

38. Hayward, ed, p. 296.

39. Corn, or the predominant grain, was wheat, rye, barley or oats in neolithic Europe.

40. McCana, pp. 27-28, and p. 90.

41. Larousse, p. 244.

42. Herm, p. 155.

43. Whistler, p. 189.

44. Walker, *Dict*, p. 186.

45. Stewart, p. 81.

46. Frazer, *Corn & Wild*, pp. 53-55.

47. Rutherford, p. 27, and Cooper, p.115.

48. Cooper, p. 115.

49. Best, *Agric*, p. 216.

50. Ihimaera, p. 197.

Autumn Equinox

Poututerangi, Ngahuru,
Seed Time and Harvest

21 – 22 March

There is a sense of calm around autumn equinox as the fine weather lingers on with seductive steadiness, making winter seem far distant. Yet shadows are beginning to lengthen and sunbeams slant under verandahs, shafting in under low windows.

In the bush houhere (lacebark) is flowering with showers of delicate white blossom. However, for the most part, flowering is over and the season moves on into seed time. Tiny, purple pate berries dangle in long fingers. Round, black capsules of putaputaweta are now forming, together with small, purple kapuka berries, rimu and totara seeds, and the beautiful, juicy kahikatea. Yellow poroporo berries hang from the bushes, orange karaka may linger on, and autumnal red clusters of nikau berries push their way out under the new season's fronds. The small, black fruit of the kaikomako attracts popokotea (whiteheads) and komako, or more commonly, korimako (bellbirds), after which the tree is named. On the bush floor the mature, round, female cones of the kauri tree fall and split open to reveal wing-like seeds, the small beginnings of forest giants to come. Along the coast black pods of harakeke (flax) lick the sky like charred flames, and burst to reveal small, black seeds that glisten in the mellow autumn sunshine.

It is a time for cutting, gathering and storage. In Britain, bracken was cut as it turned bronze and yellow, and was left on the hillsides to dry. Later it would be brought into the lofts and used for storing the apple crop. In Aotearoa, raupo was cut in March when it was at its best, and the

Summer's arrow is spent,
Stored her last tribute.
(Mary Ursula Bethell, *Dirge*).[1]

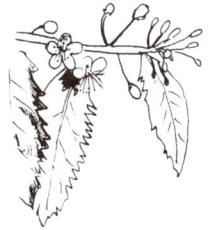

leaves used for thatching.[2] In both countries it is still berry time; in Britain blackberries, cranberries, red and black currants would be gathered for jam and wine-making; in Aotearoa karaka berries were gathered, soaked and hangi-steamed.[3]

Pine cones drop and are gathered for firewood. Chestnuts ripen and fall from the trees, sunflower heads loosen their nutty kernels. Grapes burst with purple fullness and are turned into wine; apples become rosy and abundant, the surplus being crushed to make juice. Rosehips ripen on bushes where the blooms have long since dropped.

At autumn equinox light and dark come once more into balance. It is time to give thanks and make offerings, to acknowledge the power of seeds to carry life during their time of gestation over the dark months. This is the moment to tune in to the mystery of the changeover, knowing that what appears to be a time of dying is really part of the movement forward into renewal and rebirth. This is the moment to hold faith that the darkness will bring forth new life at spring equinox.

Aotearoa

In the Maori calendar the ninth month, Huitanguru, when the foot of Ruhi, the wife of Rehua/summer rests upon the earth, has passed. It is now Poututerangi, when the crops are dug up. Poututerangi takes its name from the pole that Tane used to separate his parents Rangi and Papa. The literal meaning of Poututerangi is 'the post that lifted up the sky'.[4] This month was described as the one when *ka hauhake te kai i konei; ka ruhi te tipu o nga mea katoa* ('crops are now lifted; all growth becomes weak').[5] It was also known as Ngahuru-kai-paenga ('the food threshold of the tenth'), because food was so plentiful, or te Ngahuru hauhake kumara ('the crop-lifting tenth'), ngahuru being the old word for ten.[6] For this was the beginning of the kumara harvest, perhaps the most significant event of the year. It has been described as follows:

> Ngahuru was the harvest time when the kumera [sic] was gathered, and the Maori was happy then because there was abundance of good things to eat... He looked forward to Ngahuru, when he could get ten meals a day if he wished them, or could eat them. Yes! Ngahuru was the longest and happiest month of the year.[7]

In the Te Aitanga-a-Mahaki lullaby, He Popo, from Turanga (Gisborne) the bounty of Poututerangi is referred to:

Te ngahuru tikotikoiere,
Ko Poututerangi te matahi o te tau
(Hence the bounteous harvest time
When Poututerangi brings forth the first-fruits of the year.)[8]

Stars

Certain stars announced the moment: Poututerangi (Altair), which one Tuhoe authority described as another aspect of Rehua (Antares) the summer star: 'When his feet alight upon the earth he is called Poute-te-Rangi; this is the autumn. When but one foot has so alighted he is still called Rehua.'[9] It was thought that Poututerangi came down to earth in autumn, bringing the harvest down with him.[10] At the appearance of Poututerangi a tapu man called a mata paheru would inspect the crop to see if the kumara were fully developed, and if they were, harvest would begin.[11]

Another sign was the morning appearance of Whanui (Vega), which was greeted with joy, for this was the tohu (sign) that the

kumara could now be harvested. By this time the storage pits were ready, and Whanui gave warning not to delay because frosts could be on their way.[12]

Kumara harvest

Important rituals attended the lifting of the crop. Karakia were offered at dawn, and the first kumara to be dug were those that had been ritually planted as the first seeds in spring. These special tubers were cooked in a separate hangi and offered to Pani. In this way the tapu of Rongomatane, god of the cultivated crops, was laid to rest.[13]

A fine, sunny day was chosen for the lifting of the crop, which was done when the sun was well up and continued until it reached the zenith. Dry conditions were essential for the sorting and storage process. The tubers were carefully stacked in the rua (storage pits), interlaced with native pennyroyal,[14] and touched only by men, and women past menopause.[15]

Occasionally at harvest a big, unusually-shaped kumara would be dug up. It was called Pani's medium, or Pani's canoe because it connected Pani, the crop and the tohunga. This kumara was sacred. If eaten in the usual way Pani would be insulted and the crops would rot. Instead it was kept aside by the tohunga and later cooked on a sacred fire as part of the 'first fruits' offering. Finding such a kumara was a sign that Pani had responded to the invocations and granted her blessings, for such a kumara would appear only if the crop was a bountiful one.

After the harvest there was much feasting and celebration, with games and song and dance. This was the message of Whanui, according to one Maori: 'O friends! Here am I, Whakakorongata, awake and rise! Seize your spade, and to work; store the crop in the pits, then turn to rejoicing and sing your chants of joy, for all women and children are now joyful, there is nothing to disturb them.'[16]

Whanui and the kumara theft

Whanui was a central figure in the story of the origins of the kumara. Once there was no kumara on earth; it lived only in the sky, where it was closely guarded by the star Whanui. Down on earth Pani and her husband Rongo heard about this wonderful food in the sky. Rongo climbed up to the home of Whanui to ask for some, but Whanui refused to give up his special children, the many varieties of kumara. Rongo was not deterred. He waited until Whanui was asleep, and stole the precious tubers. Back on earth, he inserted a piece of kumara into his ure (penis) and fertilised his wife. Pani was now pregnant with the kumara crop, and when the time came she went into water and gave birth to many children, each a different variety of kumara.[17]

Rongo's theft was not without consequences, however, for Whanui avenged himself by sending three species of caterpillar down to earth to attack the crop. They have caused much trouble ever since, and a lot of work, since people had to pick them off by hand, or burn green kawakawa leaves between the rows to poison them. There are several sayings about these awheto (caterpillars), one of which is a Waiohua saying referring to the Tamaki area: *Kohi awheto ki nga mara a Te Tahuri* ('gather the caterpillar from the cultivation grounds of Te Tahuri'). These extensive gardens were around Maungakiekie (One Tree Hill) in Auckland. Being very large and productive, they attracted many caterpillars.[18] Another saying *E tupu atu kumara, e ohu e te anuhe* ('the kumara springs up and as quickly does the anuhe, i.e. awhato, or awheto') was used to compare an ungrateful person with the crop-destroying caterpillar.[19]

Another bane of the crops was the small weed parahia, referred to in the proverb, *Tena te ringa tango parahia* ('this is the hand that pulls the weed'), referring to a hard worker.[20]

Other proverbs refer to the abundance of this season: *He huanga ki matiti, he tama ki tokerau* ('a relative in the summer [when food is scarce], a son in autumn' [when food is plentiful]),[21] *Ngahuru kai hangai, koanga kai anga ke* ('at harvest eating openly, in spring eating secretly'),[22] and *Tiketike ngahuru, hakahaka raumati* ('high in autumn, low in summer'),[23] referring to the level of food supply.

Pani and Maui

Another story about Pani tells how she was shamed by Maui. Once he went out fishing with his brothers while Pani prepared food for them. It was the delicious new food, the kumara, which they enjoyed so much that they begged her to tell them where it came from. Pani refused. Then Maui decided he would find out. He hid Pani's sacred girdle, her tu whakawhanau, that she wore when she went into water to give birth to the kumara. Usually she went at night, but this time she had to wait until daybreak when Maui gave back her girdle. He hid and watched from a high vantage point overlooking the waters where she went to give birth, chanting as she did so. When Maui saw what she was doing he said, 'We are being fed with the paraheka (secretions) of Pani,' thus shaming her and causing her to go into the underworld. She took with her Hine-mataiti, mother of the kiore (rat) and there tended her kumara patch, until eventually Maui discovered her by using his magic dart.[24]

This story is strikingly similar to European tales of suppression of the powers of the feminine, many of which involve not only shaming (Susanna and the elders) but pursuit and rape (Persephone and Hades). They illustrate the repression of the ancient Goddess cultures of Europe.

The underworld story of Hine-titama is suggestive of more empowering versions of the Persephone story, which emphasise her taking on new powers as a result of her journey, when she becomes Queen of the Underworld and the guide of souls after death. Hine-titama, first-born of Tane and Papatuanuku, was goddess of the dawn. Not knowing the identity of her father, she became Tane's wife and gave birth to several daughters. One day she asked her husband, 'Who is my father?' He replied, 'Go ask the posts of the house.' On doing so, Hine-titama learned the shameful truth, and fled down the path that leads to the underworld. Tane followed, begging her to return, but she forbad him to go any further, saying, 'Go back to the world of light, Tane, and I will go into the unknown. You will rear our children in the world of light, and after death I will draw them down into the underworld, the realm of the dead, where I will take care of their spiritual welfare.' It was then that the path of death was opened, and Hine-titama became Hine-nui-te-po, goddess of death.[25]

Pagan Europe

But ah the Sickle! Golden Eares are Cropt;
Ceres and Bacchus bid good night...
(Richard Lovelace, *The Grasse-Hopper*)[26]

Celtic Europe

For the Celts of Europe, the equinoxes were less important than the other main festivals on their moon calendar. In the old Coligny calender autumn equinox spanned 'Arbitration Time' and 'Song Time'.[27] With light and dark in balance it would have been a fitting opportunity for fair judgments, and as the harvest was gathered there was much to sing about.

Anglo-Saxon Britain

The Anglo-Saxons, who colonised Britain from the fifth century onwards, called this gerst-monath, meaning 'barley month',[28] barley being the first grain grown in Britain.

Celtic Mabon

Autumn equinox is often referred to as Mabon. Mabon, son of Modron,[29] was the Celtic Apollo, the divine child of light who was associated with music, therapy, and the orders of creation. His mother, Modron, was a form of the great Mother Goddess (her name relates to that of Madrona, the Roman name for the Great Mother). So why should a time when the light balance shifts towards darkness be associated with a child of light? The story goes like this.

Mabon was stolen from his mother when he was only three days old. He was imprisoned in a dungeon, and there left in darkness. Many years later King Arthur and his knights were on a quest to hunt a giant boar, but in order to proceed were told they needed the presence of

Mabon. How could they find him after he had been lost for so long? First they asked the Ousel of Cilgwri, a bird who said Mabon must have lived before his time, and who directed the knights to the Stag of Redynvre, who was one of an earlier race of animals. The stag referred them to the Owl of Cwm Cawlwyd, whose origins were still more ancient. The owl referred them on to the Eagle of Gwern Abwy, whose heritage went back still further, and the eagle referred them to the most ancient creature of all, the Salmon of Llyn Llyw. The great salmon took a knight on each shoulder and brought them to the dungeon where Mabon was lamenting his plight. There, with Arthur's help, they freed him, and the ritual hunt was able to take place.

The time of Mabon's imprisonment is equivalent to that of the dark season which begins at autumn equinox; this is when the light of the sun is swallowed up and hidden in the dark womb/dungeon of the Goddess. The time of his liberation is spring equinox, when Mabon himself was adolescent and in the springtime of his life.[30]

Eleusinian mysteries of Greece

For the best-documented rituals of autumn equinox we need to go to Greece where the Greater Eleusinian Mysteries were held. The rituals are charged with the presence of the grain goddess Demeter, symbolised by the old corn which gives up its seed in order to give birth to new crops. Persephone, her daughter, becomes a mythical embodiment of the young corn. When Persephone descended into the underworld her distraught mother searched the earth, lamenting the loss and sending the whole earth into mourning. Exhausted, Demeter came to rest at Eleusis, and there a temple was eventually raised in her honour. Finally, through the intervention of Hecate the Crone, Persephone was released and the world burst forth into joyous flowering as Demeter's repressed energy was set free.

To the ancient Greeks, the story spoke of the journey of the soul to the underworld of Hades, god of death, and also of the possibility of rebirth and return. The rituals of the Eleusinian Mysteries took initiates on a night journey into the sacred darkness where they witnessed a profound revelation of the Goddess's powers of transformation.

Rebirth became not merely an idea, but an experience, bringing with it the deep conviction that this would happen to them after they died. As the philosopher Sophocles said, 'Thrice happy they of men [sic] who looked upon these rites ere they go to Hades's house; for they alone there have true life.'

The Mysteries were celebrated every five years, beginning at autumn equinox on 23 September, the first day of Libra. As the poet Julian said in his Hymn to the Mother of the Gods, 'The Goddess Herself chose as Her province the cycle of the equinox. For the most holy and secret mysteries of Dea [Demeter] and Kore [Persephone] are celebrated when the sun is in the sign of Libra, and this is quite natural.'[31]

Day One, 23 September, was the Day of Assembly, when all the would-be initiates gathered in Athens. Sacred objects were brought from the temple at Eleusis in carts drawn by oxen – some say by the youths of Athens, others by the matrons. In a small box or basket lay Demeter's comb and mirror, a serpentine figure, some wheat and some barley. With great ceremony it was carried into the temple known as the Eleusinian at the foot of the Acropolis.

On Day Two the mystae (faithful) bathed in the sea to purify, taking with them pigs to be sacrificed. After bathing they dressed in new linen clothes.

Day Three was the day of offering, which included barley that had been grown in a field at Eleusis.

Day Four was the solemn procession with the kalathion, the sacred basket of Demeter, carried on a cart while the people ran alongside crying out Chaire Demeter! (Hail Demeter!) Behind the carts walked the women called the kristophoroi, carrying baskets of carded wool, grains of salt, pomegranates (the fruit Persephone ate in the underworld), special cakes, a serpent, ivy boughs and sesame seeds.

Day Five was the Torch Day. As the procession arrived at Eleusis in the evening it was greeted by people running about with blazing torches, re-evoking the nine distraught days when Demeter searched the world for her lost daughter, bearing flaming torches as she went.

Day Six was named after Iacchos (a mystic name for Dionysus) who accompanied his mother with torch in hand during her search.

As people processed along the Sacred Way they paused at significant sacred places: a fig tree, then a water crossing where they drank the sacred drink kykeon, made from wheat and mint. At a second water crossing they identified themselves with a sign and a password. Then they were ready to enter the Mystike Eisodos, the Entrance of the Mysteries.

Once inside, the mystae watched a ritual drama of Persephone's journey into the underworld. The epoptae, or higher-grade initiates, attended another enactment and were witnesses to the Divine Revelation.

What did they see there in the hushed darkness? No one knows for sure, for the initiates were sworn to secrecy. However, from what has been pieced together from various sources, it may have gone something like this: A door led to a small inner chamber called the anaktoron. To the right sat the hierophant on his throne. He and the priestess of Demeter came together and enacted the symbolic sexual union of the Sky Father Zeus and the Corn Goddess Demeter. All torches were put out and the couple descended into the dark interior. After a silence filled with suspense the hierophant reappeared holding up an ear of corn in a blaze of light: the mystical fruit of the divine union. At the climactic moment he cried out, 'The noble Goddess has borne a sacred child! Brimo has borne Brimos!'[32]

Out of the darkness light was born. The sacred corn had been birthed by the goddess and the cycle of life was assured. By witnessing this, initiates had the miraculous power of the Goddess deeply imprinted on their psyche.

The Eleusinian Mysteries were so important that they were said to hold the entire human race together, according to Zosimus writing in the fourth century.[33] One thing is certain: autumn equinox, that moment when the light begins to tilt towards darkness, was not a time of gloom and despondency. Instead it was an occasion for profound initiation into the secrets of the Goddess, into the cycle of death, rebirth and life of which she was the guardian. Autumn equinox was a time of hope, of the triumph of the human soul.

Christian Europe: harvest

St Michael

No major Christian festival became attached to autumn equinox. Why was this? It would appear that there was no answering resonance in Christianity to the stories of the descent into the underworld of Mabon or Persephone. The closest Christian festival came a week later, at Michaelmas, in honour of St Michael, the chief archangel who expelled Satan from heaven. In the Northern Hemisphere this fell on 29 September. It was the traditional time to eat goose,[34] the bird that had grown fat on corn stubble left after harvest, and it was thought to be bad luck to eat blackberries on or after this day.

Harvest rites

In many country areas of Britain harvest rites survive in various customs enacted at the cutting of the rye, wheat or barley crop. The practices go back to neolithic cultures where the last ears of grain would be tied on the top of a mound to signify the umbilical cord, connecting people with the womb of the Goddess inside the earth.[35] Throughout ancient Egypt, Greece, and all over the grain-growing lands of Europe, people made corn dollies.[36] In Greece the corn seed itself was stored in pots near the hearth to remind people of the dead, known as the Demetrioi, the people of Demeter the Grain Mother, who were at rest in her womb and would be resurrected in the spring.[37]

In the practice of 'Crying the Neck' special attention is given to the cutting of the last sheaf of corn. The men gather round, and one of them shapes the last stalks into a 'corn dolly', a form which recalls the old corn goddesses. She may be dressed up as the Harvest Queen and brought in to the village on a wagon, or she may be taken to represent the Cailleach or Hag of the old year, one to be avoided. A man will run to a house to foist it upon a waiting young woman, who has to first douse him with water if her fate of receiving the Corn Hag is to be avoided.

In other places the last sheaf of corn was regarded as the embodiment of the Corn Goddess herself, and the reapers would do their best to avoid being the one to cut the last stalk. They did this by lining up and throwing their sickles at it, so the goddess would not know by whose hand she had been felled. The image made of the last stalks was taken to the harvest home feast where it took a place of honour. When the fields were ploughed just after winter solstice on Plough Monday, the goddess image would be buried in the first furrow so that fertility could be carried on from one year to the next.[38] In eastern and rural Europe a piece of bread is put into the field at the end of harvest. After the reapers have found it and circled it three times, they eat a piece and then bury the rest in the earth to ensure a good harvest for the year to come. Sometimes the bread is buried after the first spring ploughing for the same reasons.[39] These customs assert the power of continuity and the repeating cycle.

In other places the reapers might climb a hill, and holding the corn dolly up high, raise the harvest shout. In Warwickshire it went:

Up! Up! Up! a merry harvest home
We have sowed; we have mowed;
We have carried our last load[40]

And in Wiltshire:

Well ploughed,
Well sowed,
Well harrowed,
Well mowed,
And all safely carried to the barn wi' nary a load throwed!
Hip-hip-hip-hooray![41]

The harvest service

The Church readily absorbed the old pagan practices of harvest celebration, welcoming it in with the ringing of bells. People brought their wheat and bread to be blessed, and even hung a corn dolly over the chancel arch. However, none of this survived the zeal of the Reformation; it wasn't until Victorian times that the Harvest Thanksgiving service was revived, and people could once more bring the fruits of the harvest into the church to be blessed. The revival is believed to date from 1843, when Rev. R.S. Hawker invited his parishioners to come and receive the sacrament 'in the bread of the new corn' at his church at Morwenstow, in Cornwall.[42]

Rituals for today

Autumn equinox is harvest time in both Maori and European traditions, the time of plenty, when rituals of celebration take place. We bring in the fruits of the harvest, we feast, play games, and sing.

Two symbols can now sit side by side: the kumara and the ear of corn, for both are abundant. Even though corn in Europe was traditionally an ear of wheat, sweet corn or maize is readily available to us today, and carries a similar meaning. It is also time to contemplate storage of the season's goodness. At harvest, both European and Maori symbolism is surprisingly similar. The rua, or underground kumara pit, is a symbol that parallels the European imagery of the return of the seed to the earth.

This was when Persephone the Maiden, goddess of the young corn, went to dwell with Hades in his realm of death, the underworld. The story is echoed by the Maori tale of the goddess Pani, mother of the kumara, who is shamed by Maui and descends to the underworld with Hine-mataiti, mother of the kiore; and also by the story of Hine-titama who went to the underworld and became Hine-nui-te-po. The imagery is repeated again in the story of Mabon imprisoned in the dark dungeon.

At autumn equinox we might gather around the first fire, turn out the lights and listen to these stories of journeys into darkness while we grind sesame seeds with a pestle and mortar. As we listen we can contemplate the parallels with what is happening in nature: how the balance of light and dark tips at equinox, and we now enter the dying

phase of the year. It is time to contemplate the mysteries of life and death.

This is when we make the transition from outer to inner, from above to below, from light into dark. A simple way of doing this is to pass around a bowl of water or dark wine, with the words 'outer to inner, autumn is here'. Turning within gives us the opportunity to contemplate our own inner harvest to see how it contains the seed of whatever new crop is to come in spring. This is when we draw faith and prepare ourselves, contemplating the outer harvest of both cultures: kumara in the storehouses and grain in the granaries, as well as the inner harvest of our own lives. What is it that has been gathered into our inner storehouses to be drawn on during times of need? Have we replenished ourselves and harvested from life during the growing season of the year? It is a good time to share a symbol of our inner resources with others. By celebrating the equinox harvest in this way we honour our inner riches and let go of the work cycle that preceded the gathering.

The ritual is then followed by a harvest feast, of kumara and corn, with aubergines, capsicums and tomatoes simmering in a delicious ratatouille, followed by grapes, the fruit of the season.

1. Curnow, ed., p. 117.

2. Orbell, *Nat World*, p. 54.

3. Makereti, p. 210.

4. Beattie, pp. 28-29, and Graeme Murdoch, pers. comm.

5. Best, *Time*, p. 22.

6. Tikao says that it meant 'more than ten', because it referred to the last three months of the year. (Beattie, p. 45)

7. Beattie, p. 45.

8. Ngata, *Nga Moteatea II,* pp. 154-155.

9. Best, *Astron,* p. 59.

10. Orbell, *Poetry,* p. 84.

11. Simmons, p. 181.

12. Best, *Astron,* p. 64, and Makereti, p. 193.

13. Barlow, p. 102.

14. Dell Wihongi, pers. comm.

15. Best, *Agric,* p. 137 and p. 171.

16. Best, *Astron,* p. 64.

17. Best, *Astron,* p. 64, and Reed, pp. 221-222.

18. Graeme Murdoch, pers. comm.

19. Riley, 18-4.

20. Brougham, p. 29.

21. Brougham, pp. 79-80.

22. Brougham. p. 43.

23. Brougham, p. 44.

24. Best, *Agric,* p. 106.

25. Best, *Aspects,* pp. 17-18.

26. Sitwell, p. 390.

27. Matthews, p. 92.

28. Holden, p. 121.

29. Mabon, meaning 'son', and Modron, meaning 'mother', are honorific titles rather than the true names of deities. Tolstoy, p.206, suggests they may stand for real names that could not be uttered, and points out that Mabon bears many similarities to the god Lugh.

30. Stewart, p. 109, and Rolleston, pp.391-392. Compare Homer in his 'Hymn to Demeter': Happy is he among men on earth who has seen these mysteries; but he who is uninitiate and who has no part in them, never has lot of like good things once he is dead down in the darkness and gloom. (Neumann, p. 323)

31. Durdin-Robertson, p. 158.

32. Durdin-Robertson, pp. 156-167, Larousse, pp. 178f, Frazer, *Bough*, p.188

33. Durdin-Robertson, p. 158.

34. Dunkling, p. 76.

35. Gimbutas, p. 149.

36. Green, p. 54.

37. Gimbutas, p. 145.

38. Cooper, p. 128.

39. Gimbutas, p. 147.

40. Cooper. p. 129.

41. Cooper. p. 128.

42. Cooper, p. 135, and Whistler, p.193.

Last Light

*Haratua, Paengawhawha,
Samhain, Halloween*

30 April

By the end of April we begin to feel the impact of the receding light: nights are drawing in, leaves have fallen from deciduous trees and fruit has been stripped from the orchard. First frost may already have struck. Energy is being withdrawn.

In the bush, fruiting continues, with rimu, totara and tawapou now coming into berry. Horoeka (lancewood) and miro may have begun to fruit, the miro attracting tui, popokotea (whitehead) and kereru, or kukupa (wood pigeon).

Aotearoa

In the Maori year it is the eleventh lunar month, Paengawhawha, when *kua putu nga tupu o nga kai i nga paenga o nga mara* ('the refuse of food plants is piled up on the edges of the fields'). Soon the season will pass into the twelfth, Haratua, when *kua uru nga kai kai te rua, kua mutu nga mahi a te tangata* ('crops are stored in pits; labours are over').[4] The twelfth month was relatively inert now that the major event of the kumara harvest was over, and was often dropped from the calendar. However, other foods came into season: taro, where it was warm enough to grow, fern root, gourds and cabbage tree suckers.[5]

Hunting the kiore

Emphasis now shifted to the bush, the domain of Tane, as a food source. From April to August, and even to December in some parts, it was time to catch the kiore, the small, dark rat that lived on berries, including miro, hinau, kahikatea, patate, karamu, puriri, tawai, and tawa.[6] The kiore may be traced back 5000 years to South-east Asia, from where it was eventually brought by migrating seafarers to

Ehara i te uaua tangata, otira he uaua kiore.
(Not strong like a person, but weak as a rat)[1]

I write in waning May
and it is autumn.
(Mary Ursula Bethell,
'Response')[2]

So, purging our borders
We burn all rubbish up, that all
weak and waste growth,
that all unprofitable weeds,
All canker and corrosion,
May be consumed utterly.

These universal bonfires
Have a savour of sacrifice.
(Mary Ursula Bethell, 'Dirge')[3]

Polynesia and by the Maori to Aotearoa. After European settlers brought larger rats and other predators, kiore numbers declined on the mainland, and until recently it was believed by many to be extinct. However, it has been discovered in a remote corner of the South Island and on some off-shore islands, much to the joy of many Maori people. A late 19th-century proverb poignantly illustrates Maori feeling about the loss of the beloved kiore:

Ko te ao tonga o te kiore i a pouhawaiki
(Just as the introduced rat supplants the kiore)
Te ngaro o te tui i te piere
(Just as the robin supplants the tui)
Hapai ana te haeata, ko te kiritea e huna ana i te moko
(So does the Pakeha supplant the Maori).[7]

Unlike the larger, more aggressive Norway and ship rats that came to Aotearoa with European settlers, the kiore is a creature of clean habits. It was kai rangatira, a revered food for distinguished chiefs, and a companion animal honoured in waiata and carvings. Hills, mountains and even tribes were named after the kiore; for example, the Tuhoi kai kiore, who used to serve preserved kiore to visitors.[8] Places named after the kiore are the hill Parakiore, north of Whangarei, the island Motukiore in the Hokianga harbour, and the village Te Niho o te kiore (the teeth of the rat) near Te Aroha, which was named after the many hinau berries which were found imprinted with teeth-marks of the kiore.[9]

Many sayings illustrate the importance of the kiore in the everyday life of the Maori: Honoa te hono o te kiore ('assemble just as the kiore assembles'), and Ko tini o parahiore ('a swarm of rats'), which refers to a heavily populated area. The saying Ka titi kiore, ka hoki mai ('when you hear the squeak of the rat, return home') was used to remind young people to come home at dusk, when the kiore began to make itself heard.[10]

In summer the kiore was in poor condition, but it grew fat in late autumn and winter, when feed was plentiful. This creature was a descendant of the goddess Pani, whose daughter Hine-mataiti gave birth to it.[11] The kiore in turn attacked another child of Pani, the kumara, and the old men would sit all night holding flax strings threaded with shells that they shook at regular intervals to frighten the marauders away. There was also competition with the rat for tawhara, the bracts of the kiekie, flowering at Last Light and said to taste like rich, juicy pears with an aroma of vanilla.[12] The kiore loved them as much as humans did, and so the old people would tie the uppermost leaves over the bracts and fruit to prevent the rats from getting to them first.[13] Sometimes the old people left parts of the tawhara open so that the kiore could have its share.[14] Alternatively, the kiore helped itself first, preferring to eat the unripened fruit, but left a share for the human gatherers who liked to eat the tawhara ripe: 'the kiore knew how to share kai'.[15]

The kiore was an important source of food in the South Island, where one of its favourite foods, the hua tawhai (beech mast; i.e. small, brown, flaky seeds of the beech tree) grew. When the beech was having a good season, the kiore flourished. It was said that pollen from the beech flowers drifted down rivers and across the ocean, back to the homeland of Hawaiki. On receiving this signal the kiore of Hawaiki would begin their long swim to Aotearoa, where they would come to get fat on the tawhai.[16]

A folk-tale about the kiore and the kakariki (parakeet) illustrates the place of the kiore as primarily an earth-dweller, as distinct from the birds who inhabit higher realms:

> Said the kakariki to the kiore: 'O Kio! Let us ascend the trees.'
> The kiore asked, 'And what shall we do there?'
> Replied the kakariki, 'We will feed on tree berries.'
> Asked the kiore, 'What berries are they?'
> The kakariki replied, 'They are miro and kahikatea berries.'
> Then said the kiore, 'I am of the earth, of the realm of Tane, until
> human beings come and snare me by the neck.'[17]

The story illustrates a co-operative relationship between bird and kiore, similar to that reported as taking place between humans and kiore in their sharing of the tawhara. It is said that when the miro

berries were ripe, the kiore refrained from tree-climbing, for this was also the time when the birds fed on the miro. The kiore would stay on the ground, eating the berries that fell down while the birds fed in the trees above.[18] Miro berries fermented in the stomachs of both kiore and kereru (wood pigeon), making them drunk and therefore easier to catch. The berries also imparted an aromatic flavour to the kiore flesh, making it even more delicious to eat than usual.[19]

The kiore lived in holes in the ground and tree hollows by day, and came out to feed at night. They moved through the bush in single file, as referred to in the saying *Honoa te hono a te kiore* ('in single file like rats')[20] along well-defined trails known as ara kiore. Important trails were named and well known, some of them running for many miles.

At the opening of the season people moved to the bush and set up camp, each group having its defined hunting ground on which no one else would intrude. The ritual experts would consult for correct procedures, and then the huhunga or whakanoatanga (tapu-lifting ceremony) would take place. Part of this was the chanting of a tuota (a charm used to secure game) to attract the rats and then a whangai (rite with an offering to the gods).

Certain restrictions applied to the first day and night of the season. People had to fast, and could not speak until the rats were taken from the traps on the second day. Throughout the season words such as tamaiti (young person), wahine (woman) and koroheke (old man) were banned and replaced by more obscure substitutes, in case the rats would be deterred.[21]

During the night both men and women set tawhiti (traps) along the trails, clearing and re-setting them as rats were taken. At full moon all trapping ceased, for then the kiore was wary. As the proverb says, *He ata marama e kore ai e mau te kiore, he ata tangata e kore ai e mau te tangata* ('you cannot catch a rat in the moonlight, nor can you catch a man on a bright morning').[22] By day, women plucked or skinned and cooked the rats from the previous night's catch. The first rat killed would be offered to the atua (god) after a karakia had been chanted, and omens read from the way they were caught.[23] The season would now continue through the winter until the berry supply ran out.

Rat food was rich and tasty when preserved in its own fat as

huahua, and was much prized, both on its own or as a relish for fern root or kouka (cabbage-tree food).[24]

Bird hunting

The berries attracted not only rats, for this was now the threshold of the bird season. From around autumn equinox the tohunga visited the forests to see how the fruiting was going. Certain trees might be especially noted and visited every year; for example, the Rongowhakata people would carefully examine a notable kahikatea that grew inland from Gisborne as soon as its fruit had set. If most of the berries were on the seaward side it would be a good season for fish but not for birds; if on the landward side the bird season was favoured.[25]

Meanwhile, in the whare mata the men made thousands of snares from flax and cabbage-tree leaves. When the signs of readiness were there in the bush, a few test birds were snared to see if they were now good to eat; if so, the season could open. During the breeding season the birds had been protected by a rahui, signalled by a post painted with red ochre or with tufts of vegetation tied to it. Now the rahui would be lifted.[26]

Women as well as men sometimes took part in bird-snaring and were allocated certain trees with names like Kake-wahine and Piki-wahine.[27] Different whanau (family groups) had control over their own rauiri (bird preserves) and trespassing was a serious offence. The boundaries were known as wakawaka and applied to the main birds, but not less important ones or the weka.[28]

Throughout the season various restrictions applied so that the birds would not be driven away. Certain words were banned, such as titiro ('to look at'), or in the Matatua district wewete (to untie), and particular procedures followed.[29] The snarers would go about their rounds without looking back, and the catch would be hidden in a hole in the ground under leaves so as not to frighten off the living birds. In some forests, cooked food was regarded as tapu and would not be taken in.[30]

Many different methods were used, each appropriate to the season, the type of tree and the bird. It was a sophisticated art, drawing on an

immense body of knowledge built up through careful and constant observation.

Hine-mahanga, goddess of birds

Hine-mahanga (Hine the snarer) was the goddess who attracted birds, the korimako (bellbird) being the first, after which many flocked to her pua (flower). She helped select trees for the placing of snares, and such trees would be protected by rituals. It was said that Hine-mahanga was so skilled at catching birds, which she then cooked and preserved, that her husband Patea felt unworthy in comparison. When he came home and saw her success he could not bear it, and killed her.[31]

Part of the tree, representing its mauri, i.e. its life-force and fruit-fulness, would be taken and hidden nearby to make sure no one or nothing would interfere and cause the birds to leave.

The main birds were kaka, kereru (wood pigeon) and the tui, which flocked to feed on the many berry trees: hinau, miro, tawari, kahikatea, maire, taupuka (mountain snowberry), and tawa. Many smaller birds would also be taken, such as korimako (bellbirds) and tieke (saddlebacks). Karuwai (robins) were easy to kill, and piopio (native thrushes) were sometimes caught, although the Maori regarded birds such as these, which ate worms and grubs, to be inferior to the honey and berry feeders.

First offerings

The first birds to be caught were cooked in a small umu tuakaha (oven used for ritual feasts) and eaten by the tohunga as a sacred offering. This lifted the tapu for the whare mata and the men who worked in it. In some places one of the first birds was cooked to the chanting of karakia, then hung in a tree and offered to Tane, god of the forests.[32] First-fruits chants were known as taumaha and were recited to remove the tapu from the food before it was eaten. One such taumaha went as follows:

Ko [te] taumaha a Taranui-a-matenga,

Ko [te] taumaha a Puhaureroa,
Ko [te] tauma[ha] aku, a Pukoroauahi:
Ka whiwhi taumaha, ka rawe taumaha,
Rawe kai taumaha, rawe manu taumaha.

(The ritual of Taranui-a-matenga,
The ritual of Puhaureroa,
My ritual – the ritual of Pukoroauahi:
The ritual is achieved, the ritual is made good,
The ritual for food, the ritual for birds.)[33]

The bird-snarers would then eat birds cooked in an umu marae especially for them, and high-born women or women involved in the ceremonies would eat from a special umu ruahine. All the rest of the people would then feast from birds and other foods cooked in a fourth earth oven, a tukupara, and celebrate the opening of the season.[34]

Horo-i-rangi

For the Arawa tribe the goddess Horo-i-rangi looked after the fertility of forests and birds, and it was to her that the first fruits were offered. Whether foods of forest or lake, they were placed in a sacred storehouse carved out of rock beside a carved image of the goddess herself.[35]

The weka season

In the South Island the weka season now began, with people migrating to the plains, valleys or hills where weka were to be found. The men set out with dogs to catch the birds, while the women back at camp plucked, cooked and preserved them in kelp bags. This went on until just before spring equinox.[36] Weka were also snared in great numbers in April.[37]

Pagan Europe

Celtic Samhain

October 31 marks the changeover into the dark time. For the Celts this was Samhain (pronounced '*shah*-vin'), when the god of life, the Dagda, mated with the Morrigon, the goddess of death. Samhain, meaning 'summer's end', was one of the two major transitions of the year, the other being Beltane, and was marked by the rising of the Pleiades.[39] In the Northern Hemisphere Samhain was held on 31 October/1 November, when it marked the close of the harvest and the beginning of the Celtic new year. In the Coligny calendar it was known as the time of 'seed-fall'.[40] Cattle were driven into stockades for winter shelter and many were slaughtered for food because of the difficulty of keeping them alive over winter. After ritual sacrifices their blood was mixed with grain to make a kind of haggis, and feasting took place.[41] This was the start of Blotmonath, the old name for November, meaning 'Blood month'.[42]

People became uneasy and fearful at the thought of the long months ahead of darkness, cold and possible food shortages. They believed the smell of blood attracted spirits of the dead. Being a time of major transition, the veil between the worlds was once more thin. Ghosts, faeries and departed souls could emerge from the sidhs (burial mounds, pronounced 'shee') and stalk the earth, leading travellers astray or beguiling the unwary into leaving the earthly realm and joining them. It was a risky time to travel abroad. Keats's poem 'La Belle Dame Sans Merci' is derived from the old stories, and tells of attempts by the banshee, the beautiful Irish sidh-women, to lure mortal lovers into their realm. The poem makes the seasonal setting quite clear:

> O what can ail thee, knight-at-arms,
> Alone and palely loitering?
> The sedge is withered from the lake,
> And no birds sing.
> O What can ail thee, knight-at-arms,

So haggard and so woe-begone?
The Squirrel's granary is full,
And the harvest's done.

...I met a lady in the meads,
Full beautiful – a faery's child,
Her hair was long, her foot was light,
And her eyes were wild.[43]

It was a period of chaos and reversal, when people played wild tricks on one another. Chimneys were blocked with turf, cattle were headed off, doors were blocked by carts, windows were tapped on, vegetables were thrown at doors and even cabbages were thrown at notable people. Girls and boys cross-dressed and visited neighbours wearing masks in order to play tricks, imitating the activity of the faeries, goblins and witches on the etheric realm.

And there she lulled me asleep
And there I dream'd – ah! woe betide!
The latest dream I ever dream'd
On the cold hill side.

I saw pale kings and princes too,
Pale warriors, death-pale were they all;
Who cried – 'La Belle Dame sans merci
Hath thee in thrall!'

I saw their starv'd lips in the gloam,
With horrid warning gaped wide,
And I awoke, and found me here,
On the cold hill side.[44]

Irish mythology told of great sacrifices made at Samhain, when people had to surrender two-thirds of their milk, corn and children to the evil powers of the ruling Formorians. Memories of human sacrifice shivered down the spine of collective memory as the bright red blood of

slaughtered animals spurted forth. Mythologically, this was when great heroes and kings died.

In Germany and Gaul people took part in riotous processions, with the men dressing in animal masks and skins to take on the power of sacred animals.[45]

This was the feast of the dead, with storytelling and divination playing an important part; in fact it was the beginning of the story-telling season, which would continue through the dark evenings until Beltane. It was also a feast of peace and friendship, when weapons were laid down and violence put aside: the end of the warfaring season that had begun the previous Beltane. With so much danger coming from the spirit world, it may have been important for people to know that they could now count on each other. During this festival of truce accounts could be settled, contracts made and marriages take place.

Christian Europe: All Souls, All Saints, All Hallows Eve, Halloween

The Church, as with other festivals, took over the pagan Samhain, turning it into All Saints (All Hallows) on 1 November and All Souls' Day on 2 November. All Saints was set up in the ninth century to honour saints both known and unknown in an attempt to erase Samhain. In a subsequent attempt to stamp out the pagan celebrations the Abbot of Cluny instigated All Souls' Day in AD 998 to honour all who had died Christians.[46] On All Souls' Eve families stayed up, waiting for the spirits of the dead to visit, and ate small cakes known as 'soul cakes'.

To this day many Roman Catholic people in Europe and both North and South America go to cemeteries on All Souls to light candles on the graves of the dead.[47]

In the Reformation in Britain the Church retained All Saints, but removed the All Souls feast from the calendar, finding it uncomfortably pagan. However, All Souls, or All Hallows Eve lived on, with its powerful interactions with dead spirits, and later became known as Halloween. Even today the festival of Halloween continues to strike at the edge of our deepest fears.

Divination and games

Divination and trickery were a feature, with 'trick or treat' developing from the ancient Irish practice where groups of peasants went from house to house asking for food and gifts for the evening celebrations in the name of Muck Olla, an early Druid deity.[48] Many games used apples or nuts, the fruits of the season. The hazel-nut was especially important, for the hazel tree was the Celts' sacred tree of life. Apples were the Celtic fruit of the Otherworld, symbolising fertility, love, wisdom and divination.[49] Apple peel might be tossed over the shoulder so that the shape it fell in would suggest the first letter of a future lover's

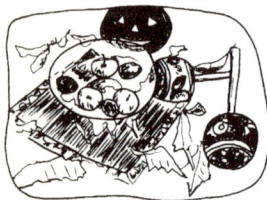

name. Apples eaten at Halloween were thought to give rise to a dream of the destined lover, hence the bobbing-for-apples game where people competed to get bites out of apples floating in water. Couples looked for a prediction about their relationship by throwing two nuts into the fire to see if they would burn steadily or explode and die. Oak apples would be placed in a bowl of water to determine the faithfulness of a lover; if they floated together it was a good sign. All this play with apples and nuts recalls the old Roman festival of Pomona on 1 November: a festival of ripening fruits when the summer stores were opened for eating.

Roman boys played a board game whose symbolism spoke of the changeover between the Maiden (the Celtic Brigit) and the Crone (the Celtic Cailleach) at this season. The hag at one end of the board let loose a dragon, and the maiden at the other end a lamb. The lamb defeated the dragon, but then the hag let loose a lion who defeated the lamb. Thus the hag reigned supreme for the season of darkness.[50]

Soul cakes

Families baked 'soul cakes' or children went 'souling' for cakes or money by singing a song. In northern England a different sort of cake was made for each family member, these cakes having the magical power to grant a wish. In Ireland people put out food offerings for the ghosts and faeries, and in England they left wine for the souls of the dead, who were believed to visit at midnight on Halloween. Candles were left lit in every room to guide the visitors. In the Isle of Man people believed the souls of the dead visited their relatives at Halloween, so left the door unlocked that night and set food out on the table.

Witches

Spells were invoked against witches. People carried torches to protect them against evil, and in Scotland bonfires were lit to scare witches away, or to burn any witch who might be hovering in the air on her broomstick. A witch effigy might even be burned outright, a custom that continued till recent times. There is a vivid account of Queen

Victoria watching a hideous witch effigy being flung on a bonfire at Balmoral, to the screeching of bagpipes.[51] These incidents speak of the twisting of the old traditions under Christian influence; in ancient times the witch was the wise woman: the Cailleach, or Hecate the Crone, goddess of death, who was welcomed as the guide to the underworld. It is Hecate who guides the Maiden Persephone through the realm of Hades and teaches her the secrets of the deep. Hecate with her sacred black cat represents the moon in her waning phase and has knowledge of the energy of withdrawal; she represents a phase of the Goddess as necessary as birth and life. However, under Christianity the power of this aspect of the Goddess was suppressed and she became a grotesque distortion that was to be feared. The witch today reflects back to us, jeeringly, our fear of death and inability to contain it within the cycle of being. Social rejection and mocking of older women is but another aspect of this.

Halloween lanterns

In Scotland and northern England people would dress as spirits, ghosts, witches and punkies, and blacken their faces in bonfire ash for protection. They lit candles in hollowed-out turnip lanterns to evoke eerily the dead revisiting earth. Later in the United States these gave way to pumpkin lanterns, which were made popular in the late 1800s by Irish immigrants who brought the festival of Halloween with them.

Medieval processions

Medieval celebrations ended with a procession, going three times around the hall, each person holding a lighted candle set in an apple. After the feast people kept the candles lit for several minutes to make sure evil spirits were scared off and the good souls cheered.[52]

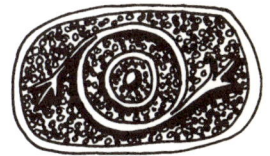

Bonfires

The bonfire was a feature of Halloween that went back to early times, and it was often lit on the top of a burial mound. As at Samhain, it was

literally a 'bone-fire', for people burned bones to produce a strong-smelling smoke that they believed had a purifying effect. Cattle would be driven through it as they came in from the fields for winter shelter. In ancient Ireland a new fire was lit every year on Samhain eve and all the fires in Ireland were then kindled from that sacred flame.[53]

Guy Fawkes' Day

Later the bonfire symbolism was transferred to Guy Fawkes' Day, in commemoration of a 1605 piece of mischief well in keeping with the old customs – though attempting to set fire to Parliament was somewhat more serious than throwing cabbages at public figures.

In his novel *The Return of the Native*, Thomas Hardy writes of the bonfire custom as it survived in 19th-century Dorset:

Red suns and tufts of fire one by one began to arise, flecking the whole country round. They were the bonfires of other parishes and hamlets that were engaged in the same sort of commemoration. Some were distant, and stood in a dense atmosphere, so that bundles of pale straw-like beams radiated around them in the shape of a fan. Some were large and near, glowing scarlet-red from the shade, like wounds in a black hide…Perhaps as many as thirty bonfires could be counted within the whole bounds of the district…

It was as if these men and boys had suddenly dived into past ages, and fetched therefrom an hour and deed which had before been familiar with this spot. The ashes of the original British pyre which blazed from that summit lay fresh and undisturbed in the barrow beneath their tread. The flames from funeral piles long ago kindled there had shone down upon the lowlands as these were shining now. Festival fires to Thor and Woden had followed on the same ground and duly had their day. Indeed, it is pretty well known that such blazes as this the heathmen were now enjoying are rather the lineal descendants from jumbled Druidical rites and Saxon ceremonies than the invention of popular feeling about Gunpowder Plot.

Moreover to light a fire is the instinctive and resistant act of man when, at the winter ingress, the curfew is sounded throughout Nature.

It indicates a spontaneous, Promethean rebelliousness against the fiat
that this recurrent season shall bring foul times, cold darkness, misery
and death. Black chaos comes, and the fettered gods of the earth say,
Let there be light.[54]

In 18th-century Wales people placed white marked stones in the dying
embers of the big Halloween bonfire. Woe betide anyone whose stone
could not be found in the morning, for according to the folklore they
would die before the next Halloween.[55]

In Jersey a large baulk of wood was dressed in human clothing and
burned on the last day of the old year, recalling the older practice of
human sacrifice. They called the figure le vieux bout de l'an, a name
that became shortened to boudelou, meaning 'guy'. This practice, too,
was later transferred to Guy Fawkes' Day.[56]

Rituals for today

Halloween on 30 April has the potential to be one of the most powerful of the seasonal festivals, yet today in this country we merely
play-act Halloween, keeping ourselves well distanced from its true
meaning. We have imported it straight from the United States without
making the seasonal translation necessary from Northern to Southern
Hemisphere. Hence we are left with the absurdity of celebrating the
festival of the dead in springtime, when all of nature is coming alive.
To restore the real meaning of Halloween we need to celebrate it on 30
April, when all of nature appears to be dying and the time of darkness
is upon us. We would be mindful of the old Samhain, when cattle were
brought in for wintering over, and people prepared themselves for the
time of bitter cold and scarcity of fresh food. Sheep and cows were dry,
hens had ceased to lay, the harvest had been brought in and the land
lay fallow. This was when people faced their fears of ageing, death
and decay. Who knows which of them would be carried away by
death during the season of long nights? It was recognised as a major
seasonal shift that dislocated time and space, opening people to other

realities. It also marked the beginning of a new year.

In our country today things are not as different as we might think. Old people get injections against the new, virulent strain of flu that might carry them away in the coming winter, the poor dread the cold nights when they cannot afford the electricity to keep warm, and over all of us hang many fears of destruction, including that of the longest night of all, the nuclear winter. Our ability to insulate ourselves physically against the weather is no protection from the age-old anxieties that the season evokes. Many people today still fear the coming of winter. Underneath our known fears lie the unspeakable ones: the great taboos of death and ageing, and the rejection of the power of the feminine in its Crone phase.

In both ancient Celtic and Maori culture this was different. An old Celtic burial site contains the grave of an elderly priestess whose body is surrounded by dozens of gold ornaments. In Maori culture both past and present, the ageing woman, the kuia, is venerated for her wisdom and acknowledged for her power.[57] The processes around dying are embraced in the rituals of the tangihanga. Te po (night of death) is faced and named. Kawakawa, a plant symbolising death and mourning, is resonant with this season: on the marae a coffin is greeted by mourners with a powhiri (action chant of welcome) in honour of the dead:

He aha te tohu o te ringaringa?
He kawakawa!
He aha te tohu o te ringaringa?
He kawakawa!
Aa, e tuku ki raro kia hope ra
E horo kia ho, te whakatau a te mate!

What is the sign in our hands?
It is kawakawa leaves (for mourning)
What is the sign in our hands?
It is kawakawa leaves
Lower them to the waist
Let them fall, death alights![58]

By celebrating Halloween in late autumn where it belongs we are more likely to open to its full meaning and to cross this important seasonal threshold with consciousness.

For the ancient Maori this was the season to venture into the realm of Tane to hunt birds and the kiore, the burrow-dweller who came out to feed on dark nights, avoiding the light of the full moon. The kiore, child of Hine-mataiti, offers us an indigenous symbol for the power of the season of Last Light, of Halloween, when creatures of darkness come out to feed.

From European culture come the fruits of the season, all of which are freely available at the end of April: apples of all kinds, nuts, pumpkins and butternuts, speaking to us of mellowness, ripeness, storage of summer warmth and goodness. Joining with them is the kumara, whose nutritious sweetness was at this time traditionally stored in underground pits on bracken and manuka brush. For this is the season when our stored ripeness is all: we need this to draw on during the months ahead, whether it be the fruits of our own experience or the wisdom of the elders, the crone, the grandmother and the kuia.

When we take a pumpkin or butternut, hollow it out and carve a grinning face, then light a candle inside it on 30 April, the orange flesh glows eerie and warm in the dark. We light up our own fears, we face Halloween, and we tread the edge of darkness both strengthened and aware.

A contemporary Last Light, Halloween or Samhain ritual would be the late autumn ritual that it is meant to be. We would draw on the symbolism of storage: kumara in the dark rua, apples, nuts, and pumpkins, and taste the flesh of these fruits of the earth. Pumpkin and kumara soup would warm the belly with the resources of both cultures.

We would gather at night and face into our darkness. It is time to hear the story of Hine-nui-te-po, goddess of death. Maui, after conquering the sun and succeeding with many other exploits, decided it was time to conquer death. He travelled west with his companions the birds, to where the goddess lay sleeping. If he could creep between her legs and enter her body through her vagina, reversing the journey of birth, and come out of her mouth, then Hine-nui-te-po would die and

humans would live forever.

At first Maui considered taking on the form of a kiore, but tataeko the whitehead said that wouldn't work. He considered changing himself into a toke, or earthworm, to enter Hine-nui, but tiwaiwaka the fantail (an insect-eater) did not approve. So Maui changed himself into a moko-huruhuru, a small, glistening caterpillar. As he began to wriggle into Hine-nui, his movements looked so ridiculous that tiwaiwaka the fantail could restrain itself no longer, and burst into laughter. Hine-nui awoke and Maui was suffocated to death.

The story tells of the foolishness of trying to conquer death. Death is part of the law of the Great Goddess, who knows it is necessary to surrender to the darkness in order to be reborn. At Halloween we honour death, and we remember the dead, perhaps by lighting a black candle for them, or by chanting or speaking their names. Maybe we could bring a photograph of those we specially wish to remember on this night.

We might honour the crones, the kuia, the wise women in our lives, reclaiming them from the darkness by naming them, thanking them, including them in our rituals, or bringing them gifts. This is the time to write a letter or send a crone card of thanks to such women. Perhaps this should be grandmother day, crone day or kuia day.

We might consider the forest and the hunting season of the ancient Maori who at this time went into the realm of Tane in search of birds and kiore. This could be the time to make a night journey into the bush, listening to the sounds of the wild creatures, taking time alone, facing into the dark. We could remember the kiore, child of Hine-mataiti, the night creature of the underground, and in doing so, remember what lies in our own underground, our own depths, to emerge and be faced at this season of changeover, the new year of the ancient Celts, and the threshold of the new year of the Maori.

1. Riley, p. 26-1.

2. Curnow, ed., p. 115.

3. Curnow, ed., p. 117.

4. Best, *Time*, p. 19.

5. Taro did not grow as well here as it had in the islands. Tikao tried it on Banks Peninsula for four years, but gave up, saying it wasn't worth the trouble (Beattie, p. 139). Makereti says it was an important food in Arawa ceremonies, such as a tangi for a tangata rangaitira (man of rank) or a significant hakari (feast) at the marae (Makereti, pp. 214-215).

6. Makereti, p. 252, and Roberts, 'Scientific Knowledge', p. 41.

7. Roberts, 'Scientific Knowledge', p.43.

8. Roberts, 'Scientific Knowledge', p. 43.

9. Roberts, 'Scientific Knowledge', p.40.

10. Roberts, 'Scientific Knowledge', p.39.

11. Best, *Forest*, p. 356.

12. Faeries were sometimes said to live in the kiekie (Orbell, p. 60).

13. Best, *Forest*, pp. 55 and 360.

14. Roberts, 'Scientific Knowledge', p. 4.

15. Manga Tau, Ngai Tawake ki te waoku, speaking in Bradford Haami's film, *Kiore*, 1992.

16. Best, *Forest*, pp. 361-362.

17. Best, *Forest*, p. 356. In another version of the tale, the rat is asked to descend in order to feed on the berries.

18. Manga Tau, Ngai Tawaki ki te waoku, speaking in Bradford Haami's film, *Kiore*, 1992.

19. Roberts, 'Scientific Knowledge', p. 41.

20. Best, *Forest*, p. 357.

21. Best, *Forest*, p. 365.

22. Riley, 17-4.

23. Makereti, p. 253.

24. Roberts, p. 43.

25. Best, *Forest*, p. 127.

26. Best, *Forest*, p. 132.

27. Best, *Forest*, p. 239.

28. Beattie, p. 136.

29. Best, *Forest*, p. 142.

30. Beattie, p. 74

31. Best, *Forest*, p. 15.

32. Best, *Forest*, p. 267.

33. Orbell, *Folktales*, pp. 60-61.

34. Best, *Forest*, p. 148-152.

35. Phillips, p. 146.

36. Best, *Forest*, p. 177.

37. Beattie, p. 134.

38. Hayward, ed, p. 284.

39. Stewart, p. 62.

40. Matthews, p. 92.

41. Slade, p. 26.

42. Holden, p. 152.

43. Keats, p. 249, verses I, II, and IV.

44. Keats, p. 250, verses IX - XI.

45. Cooper, p. 191.

46. *Ency. Brit.*, Vol II, p. 107.

47. Matthews, p. 84.

48. *Encyc. Brit.*,II, p. 107.

49. Cooper, p. 190.

50. Matthews, p. 85.

51. Harrowven, p. 90.

52. Cosman, p. 86.

53. Frazer, p.830.

54. Hardy, *Native*, pp. 16-18.

55. Walker, *Dict*, p. 527

56. Rutherford, p. 24.

57. She is evoked in the poem 'Kuia' by Patricia Bell:
Old woman with sepia skin
Carved lines down her cheeks,
With iron-grey hair
Pinned in knot behind...(Orbell, p. 94)

58. Anne Salmond, *Hui*, pp. 181-182.

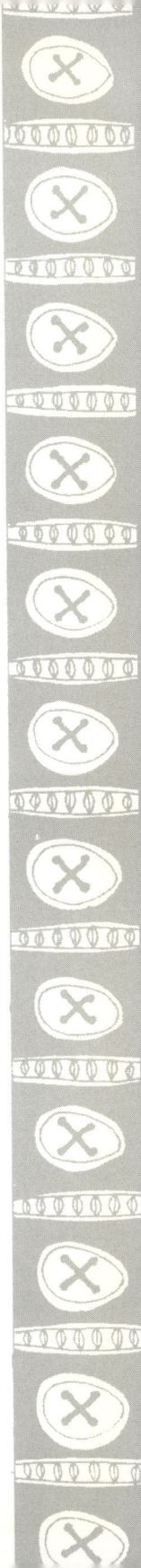

Seasonal rituals for the year: summary

Season	Setting	Theme	Colours	Goddesses gods, and celestial beings	Food
Winter solstice, Te Maruaroa o Takurua, Te Hotoke	Cave, dark room, tree decorated with images of native birds, miro berries, puriri flowers, sun and star symbols and candles	Rebirth of sun and Matariki; celebrating the turning point; Ra the sun god begins to move towards Hine-raumati, guardian of land foods. Christmas	Black, earth colours, and evergreens	Papatuanuku, Gaea, Sun god as the Divine Child; Hine-raumati; Puanga, Takurua, Matariki	Game birds, dried and pre-served foods, sun feast
First Light, Brigid, Candlemas, Pakawera, Hongonui	Inside, with candles and first spring flowers	New begin-nings, women's gatherings; puberty rituals for young women	White, yellow, orange, green	Brigid, Persephone returned from the Under-world; Mahuika, Hine-ahu-one, Tautoru and Rauroha; Kopu, Parearau	Milky foods, yoghurt, white-bait, 'lambs wool' drink
Spring equinox, Eostre, Te Koanga Te Mahuru	Outside, by newly dug earth, or on a high hill	Digging and planting; seed-ing the earth; greening of hope, Easter; resurrection	Red	Eostre, Rongomatane, Pani-tinaku; Attis/Osiris/Adonis/Christ resurrected	Dyed eggs, sprouts, karengo, hot-cross buns
Flowering and Sap-rise, Beltane, Whiringanuku	Outside, around a tree or maypole; or beside stream, pool or spring; manuka and fragrant spring flowers used as decoration	Rising sexual and creative energies; green-ing of the earth; healing and cleansing with water or fire	Green	Green Man, Attis, Tane, vegetation gods; Pan and Flora	Asparagus, salads, kiwi fruit and other green foods of the season

Season	Setting	Theme	Colours	Goddesses gods, and celestial beings	Food
Summer solstice, Te Maruaroa o te raumati	Outside, on beach or in garden, with roses, pohutu-kawa or harakeke flowers	Turning of the sun; ripening, manifestation, consummation. Ra begins to turn towards Hine-takurua, guardian of sea foods	Red, (white, yellow)	Tawhaki, Maui and the sun; Sun King; Hine-takurua, Mahuika; Parearohi, Rehua, Ruhia and Whaka-onge-kai	Sun feast: red, orange and yellow fruits and vegetables, sea food and round solstice honey cake
First Fruits/ Lean Time Lugnasad, Lammas, Te Waru	Outside in orchard, field, or inside with altar divided into two	Half Harvest; first corn, berries, and Te Waru, the lean time	Golden; dry earth colours	Lugh; Corn Mother becomes the Crone; Uruao	Bread, corn, berries, rata honey
Autumn equinox, Mabon, Poututerangi, Ngahuru	Inside, by first fire of season; ears of corn and basket of kumara	Harvest celebration; storing the goodness	Autumn colours	Pani, Hine-titama, Persephone, Mabon in the underworld; Poututerangi, Whanui	Kumara, corn, ratatouille, grapes; harvest meal
Last Light, Samhain, Halloween, Haratua	Inside in dark room; kawakawa leaves	Halloween; feast of the dead; passing into darkness; reclaiming the Crone	Black	Hine-nui-te-Po; Crone, Cailleach, kuia, Hecate; Hine-mataiti, mother of the kiore, Hine-mahanga, Horo-i-rangi	Apples, pumpkins, nuts and seeds

Celtic traditions and cosmology

Emergence of the Celts

The Celts emerged in Europe as a distinct group around the Rhinelands by about 1000-500 BCE and arrived in Britain from north-east France about 700-500 BCE. By the first millennium BCE they were regarded by the Greeks as one of the three biggest 'barbarian' nations in the Mediterranean, and were referred to as the Keltoi. By 387 BCE they had attacked Rome and even reached into Greece. In the third century BCE they plundered the Oracle at Delphi, an event that reverberates through Celtic myth with its stories of a raid on the underworld in search of magical objects or powers. Later this would become the search for the Holy Grail.

Celtic appearance and dress

The Celts were of striking appearance, tall, fair-skinned with red or blond hair, excellent horse-riders and charioteers. They wore animal-skin garments and would sit on the ground on wolf or dog skins. The men were fierce warriors who went to battle naked, letting out terrifying yells, with their shoulder-length hair matted and bleached with a lime mixture so that it stuck out in spikes like nails. The women, according to the Roman writer Diodorus, were 'not only as tall as the men but as courageous'.[1] They wore their hair long, curled or elaborately plaited and caught in gold or silver ornaments. Their hair was considered a vitally important feature. Both sexes wore magnificent woollen cloaks that were famous for their brightly coloured, striped or checked designs.

Role of Celtic women

The Celts emerged out of the neolithic cultures of Europe where the power of the feminine was revered. Women had equal rights with men, the warrior Queen Boudica being but one of many women of power.

She was described as 'enormous of frame, terrifying of mien, and with a rough, shrill voice. A great mass of bright red hair fell down to her knees: she wore a huge twisted torc of gold, and a tunic of many colours, over which was a thick mantle held by a brooch. When she grasped a spear, it was to strike fear into all who observed her.'[2]

Celtic economy

When Julius Caesar came to Britain in 55 BCE he found a large population, the ground densely studded with dwellings, many cattle, and fortified hilltops. Maiden Castle and Cadbury Castle (later 'Camelot') in Somerset are examples of these.

Celtic society was successful and sophisticated. The economy was based on three main sources of wealth:

• Farming, with pigs, cattle, sheep and horses. Wealth was
  measured not in land ownership but in head of cattle.

• Agriculture. The Celts with their skill in metalwork made tools
  to fell the forests and developed the plough to bring the land into
  productivity for crops, developing new grains and sophisticated
  herb cultivations. Grain was stored in deep, sunken silos lined
  with basket-work.

• Tolls taken from travelling merchants who needed to pass through
  strategic positions held by the Celts on major trading routes.

Along the coast they gathered shellfish, but their main foods were meat and milk. Grain production was less important in Britain than in Europe.

Warfare was common, with a lot of intertribal fighting, mostly triggered by cattle-raiding. The life of a warrior was heroic for a Celtic man, and to die gloriously in battle the highest consummation.

Seasonal cycles and the Pleiades

Being originally a mainly pastoral society, the cycle associated with the

sun and growth of crops was not as important as the cycle associated with the raising of cattle. During the winter months when feed was short and the weather cold the animals had to be brought in under shelter. In spring they would be released again for the warm season. These events divided the year into two, marked by the spring festival of Beltane at the beginning of May, the time of 'cattle-out', and the autumn festival of Samhain at the beginning of November, the time of 'cattle-in' and the beginning of the Celtic year. Both were signalled by the setting and rising of the Pleiades, seven stars which were as important to the Celts as they were to other cultures throughout the world, including that of the Maori. Each of the Pleiades relates to a different goddess and these seven maidens, said to be chased across the sky by the giant Orion, appeared in many Celtic and Greek myths.[3]

The Greeks and Romans both dated the beginning of summer from the rising of the Pleiades just before dawn in May, and farmers of ancient Greece reaped their corn then. The beginning of winter was ascertained from the Pleiades' dawn setting in November, and the farmers ploughed their fields at this time. The Roman writer Pliny dated these two events as taking place on 10 May and 11 November.[4] The Celts acknowledged the Pleiades with dance dramas about death and rebirth, some of which are still enacted today (see the account of the Padstow hobby horse, in the chapter 'Flowering and Sap-rise').

The times midway between Beltane and Samhain were the other important fire festivals, known as Imbolc and Lugnasad. However, although the lighting of fires was important at all these festivals, the moon played as important a role as the sun, just as it did in the neolithic cultures that predated the Celts. Equally important were the stars, which the Celtic priests, the Druids, used to study and discuss at length. Their knowledge was great, and comparable with that of the Greek priests and the Maori tohunga.

Moon

The Celtic calendar reflects a moon-focused consciousness, where time was reckoned not in days but in nights that went from one sunset to the next. A month began at full moon, and was further divided into two, the surviving term 'fortnight' referring to the 14-night division. Even though there were goddesses and gods associated with the sun, such as Brigid and Bel or Belenos, theirs is an inner light of divine inspiration rather than a literal sun connection.

Coligny calendar

In the late 19th century an engraved bronze calendar was discovered in fragments at Coligny in the north of France. Thought to be the work of Celtic priests, it is now known as the Coligny calendar and constitutes one of the oldest examples of Celtic writing. When pieced back together it revealed much about the Celts' way of measuring time.

Both lunar and solar cycles are recorded. Times of the year, seasons and phases of the moon are divided into auspicious or inauspicious. There are 12 months to a year, with a thirteenth month being added from time to time to bring the calendar back in line, since reckoning the year by lunar months leaves 12 days left over for every year. One intention of the calendar is to reconcile the lunar and solar cycles. To do so it takes a 19-year (Metonic) cycle which is the length of time it takes for the sun and moon to align once more. This system is similar to that used by the ancient Babylonians.

Cosmology

Celtic cosmology recognised three overlapping worlds:

● The sky world: the realm of gods and goddesses of the upper world, the sun, moon and stars. It was in this realm that the Druids saw visions and went on spirit flight.

● The earth world: the realm of humans, animals and gods and goddesses of the land and nature.

● The underworld: the realm of ancestral beings, departed human souls, gods and goddesses of death, life and rebirth. As in Maori culture, this realm was linked with the stars on a vibrational level.

(This is similar to the shamanic idea of the upper world, middle world and lower world, and in fact the Druids were shamans, female as well as male, who could enter the Otherworld by going into trance states.)

The earth zone was further differentiated. It overlaps the other two and contains elements of each of the three worlds as follows:

- **The upper earth zone** contains the movement of weather and divination based on the flight of birds. The Celts watched birds constantly for omens, and listened to their calls.

Water birds were associated with the sun, and the cormorant, duck or goose were thought to pull the sun across the sky. The eagle and swan were important birds, as was the much-dreaded crane, the form taken by hostile goddesses. It was taboo to eat the flesh of this bird. The other feared bird was the raven, which was seen as dangerous and deceitful, one that needed to be propitiated with suitable rituals.

- **The middle earth zone** contains the four directions north, south, east and west, each associated with a different element.

The four elements

The four powers or elements were important in the Druid universe and are still invoked in Wiccan rituals today. Each is associated with a particular direction, time of day, season and symbol as follows:

earth	law/north/winter/night	Stone (shield or mirror)
air	life/ east/spring/dawn	Sword
water	love/west/autumn/evening	Cauldron or cup
fire	light/south/summer/noon	Spear

The fifth direction was the unifying principle of balance at the centre.[5]

These directions became geographical fact, for ancient Ireland was divided into four provinces and a fifth in the centre, each with its own power. England, Wales and Scotland are thought to have been divided in similar fashion.

The land

In the middle earth zone there is a strong connection with the land and its features. Trees were revered, especially the ash, rowan (in Ireland), yew (in Britain), oak (throughout Gaul and Galatia) and the mistletoe that grew on it.[6] Every tribe or group of tribes had its own sacred tree which marked the site where kings were inaugurated.[7] To cut down one of these trees was a serious offence. People gathered for rituals within earthworks containing wooden temples or sacred poles, and also in sacred groves or at the site of wells and sacred waters. Where a revered tree grew over a spring or well, the site held great power, for the underworld, earth and Overworld of sky and stars is then powerfully connected. Wells are protected by the Triple Goddess and pieces of coloured cloth and written prayers are still hung around certain wells today in Ireland, Scotland and Brittany to invoke healing. Red, the ancient hue of life, is still a favoured colour for the fluttering cloth fragments.[8] There were few constructed shrines or images before the Roman occupation of Britain: the land was sufficient, for in Celtic cosmology the land, the forces of nature and all living things, and human beings, were connected and in harmony. This is reflected in the decorative patterns of Celtic art which is full of vitality and curving, interlocking shapes. The spiral appears constantly, merging into a face and then back again. Other repeating motifs reflect the energy patterns of the universe, similar to those inscribed in pottery in early Goddess-centred cultures: the whorl, lozenge, chevron, cross-hatch and angular, geometric shapes.[9]

The sacredness of the land was a central part of Celtic cosmology and the great Goddess of ancient times lived on as a goddess of sovereignty, representing the power of the land itself. Her daughter goddesses directed the evolution of human culture. Each tribe had its local goddess in whose name they would go to battle against other tribes.

The mother of the goddesses was a powerful embodiment of the polarities of life and death, fertility and war, giving and taking, creating and destroying, just as she was in ancient times. Her sons the heroes were sun gods such as Bel, Oenghus and Mabon, and eventually the Celtic Christ, as well as gods of the underworld.

All these concepts were expressed through an oral tradition in which eloquence was admired and storytelling was rich and poetic. The Celts loved song and chanting, and would keen at funerals, a practice that continues in the Irish wake.

- **The lower earth zone** taps into the underworld through burial mounds, shafts or caves. Often water is the connecting element, as in wells, sacred springs, or lakes in which treasure was often buried. This is the realm of faeries and the Cailleach, who was both the Crone and the Dark Goddess.

Head as sacred

The head was considered sacred, for it contained the soul. Heads were severed before burial and often placed in niches around doorways or mounted on spikes above houses after being preserved with cedar oil. The severed head has been compared with the Christian cross in terms of the reverence it evoked. Many shrines contained sacred heads, reflecting the fact that ancestors were revered. Skulls were often used as drinking vessels and associated with sacred wells, from where the water was drawn.

Druids

The Celtic priests were known as Druids, a word that comes from Greek drus, which is part of the Celtic word for oak, plus wid, the Indo-European word meaning 'to know'. So a Druid is the wise person of the sacred oak.[10] Their rituals usually took place at night. Three was the sacred number and the colours red, black and white the sacred colours, as in the ancient traditions, red being the colour of the Otherworld and the Great Goddess, with the polarity of black and white featuring in many Celtic legends.[11]

Druid knowledge was carefully guarded and not written down. The training consisted of 19 years of teaching so that everything could be mastered and memorised. An initiate would first learn the art of the bard, philosophy and law. Then followed seven years learning the secret language of the poets. Finally genealogy and the learning of events and laws in poetic forms completed the training.[12] The Druids were political leaders and law-givers, as well as healers and seers who held a powerful body of orally learned chants and incantations. It has often been pointed out that they bear many similarities to the Indian Brahmins.[13] We might also compare them with the Maori tohunga, for the sacred authority they hold.

Roman colonisation

Roman colonisation and the coming of literacy seriously eroded the Celtic oral tradition. In AD 61 the Romans attacked an important Druid centre at Anglesey, burning the Druid priests to death and felling their sacred groves. For the next 400 years Druidism was banned, but their traditions lived on in the bards, those highly esteemed storytellers who could travel freely across tribal boundaries.[14] It is through the mythology and stories that Druidism lives on today.

Maori traditions and cosmology

Migration and adaptation

For 80 million years Aotearoa lay isolated in the south Pacific, a land covered with dense, green forest, teeming with bird and fish life, but empty of mammals (apart from pekapeka the native bat) and, most significantly, of human beings. Then this rich and varied land was discovered by Polynesian explorers, the Maori, over 1000 years ago. Migration by large, ocean-going canoes followed, giving rise to the many tribal groups whose genealogy may still be recited today.

The new migrants were faced with a land very different from the tropical islands they had left behind. The climate was much cooler, and they were called upon to adapt in radical ways. For one thing, the tropical plants that they brought over in the canoes would not grow here: coconuts, breadfruit, sugar cane, bananas and pandanas. The aute (paper mulberry) that they grew in the islands for bark-cloth clothing was no longer easy to cultivate, and nor were the staple crops of yam and taro, except perhaps in the north of the North Island. Gourds could still be cultivated for food and vessels, but both gourds and taro had their southern limit somewhere around Nelson. Not only did kumara have a southern limit around Banks Peninsula, but it could not be grown by the old methods anywhere but in the far north. Back in the islands it had been a crop that grew all year round without difficulty. Here in the cooler climate of Aotearoa it died in winter and the seed tubers could not survive frost unless they were stored in specially insulated conditions.

Sources of protein

Radical adaptations were called for if a staple crop was to be established. Fortunately seafood was plentiful, and provided sufficient food during the initial stage when attempts to grow crops in the accustomed ways were largely unsuccessful. Sea fish provided the most important source of protein during this time, with snapper being the main North Island fish, and barracouta, followed by red cod, in the South Island.

During the first five centuries seals provided an important source of red meat, supplemented by moa, especially in the South Island.

By the 15th century moa and seals were becoming scarce, and the kuri, the native dog, fish and shellfish were relied on more. Coastal birds were also eaten, especially shags, penguins, ducks, petrels, rails, and later mutton-birds.[15] For tribes moving inland, forest birds could also be hunted.

Kumara

Crop-growing entered an experimental stage when the failure of traditional island crops meant that the new climatic conditions had to be carefully studied. Eventually a new approach to kumara growing was established, allowing life to become more stable. As a result of radical adaptation, the kumara was transformed into an annual crop with a seasonal cycle, being planted in spring and harvested in autumn. For this to be made possible the people had had to develop a sophisticated storage system in warm, insulated, underground pits so that both seed and food tubers could survive through the winter. By the time of Cook's first visit in AD 1769 this method of kumara cultivation was common and the seasonal cycle well established.[16]

Fern root and other crops

The new land offered other sources of food, fern root being the great staple that could be dug for most of the year; hence the proverb *Ka ora karikari aruhe, ka mate takiri kaka* ('fern root diggers have good health, while parrot snarers die').[17] In another proverb it is *Te tutanga te unuhia* ('the portion that can never be withdrawn'), being always available.[18] It was a symbol for war, just as kumara was the symbol for peace, fern root being the main food for war parties when they journeyed away from home.[19] An 18th-century Pakeha account considered it to be 'what bread is to us ... the foundation of all their meals'.[20] The roots were at their best in spring and early summer, and once dried would keep indefinitely. In places like Totaranui (Queen Charlotte Sound) where no gardens were observed during Cook's visit in 1769,

fern root was the most important food.[21] The pith of mamaku (black tree fern) was another fibrous food, which together with fern root was associated with the ancestor Toi te huatahi (the firstborn). Because he arrived in Aotearoa before kumara was cultivated, he was totally dependent on forest supplies.[22] He is often referred to as Toi kai rakau (Toi the eater of forest foods), and is referred to in the following song lines:

Ki nga kai a Toi, i mahue i muri ra
Te aruhe, te mamaku, te pou o te tangata e!
(For the foods of Toi, who left behind him
The fern root, and the tree fern, sustenance for humankind!)[23]

The large, sweet root of the cabbage tree also supplied starchy food, especially in the South Island where the kumara was harder to grow.[24]

Forest foods

After the kumara harvest in autumn, the forest season began with the fruiting of native trees. Whole families went out to gather berries, which they ate either raw or cooked, depending on the species. Through May, June and July birds that came to feed on the fruiting trees were snared in great numbers, a sophisticated array of methods being used. Kaka and kereru (wood pigeon) were the main birds, with tui also important, and in the South Island weka, titi (muttonbird) and ducks. The bush resounded with a flourishing bird life, in numbers hard for us to imagine now. The coming of the European changed all that, for they brought with them rats and dogs, threatening the bird life. They also brought the honey bee. There were no swarming honey bees originally, and nectar was freely available for birds, but now that there was competition bird numbers suffered a huge decline.[25]

Winter was also the season for catching the kiore, the native rat, whose flesh was tasty and nutritious.

Two food baskets

Maori people talk of two main food baskets, symbolised by the two wives of the sun god Ra. At summer solstice, when the light begins to decrease, he begins to approach his winter wife Hine-takurua, who has domain over the food basket of the ocean, and the summer fishing seasons take place. Winter solstice begins his journey towards his other wife Hine-raumati, who governs the food basket of the land, and from this point the season moves into cultivation time and the gathering of land foods.

Many proverbs compare the two food baskets: *He wha tawhara ki wa, he kiko tamure ki tai* ('the edible flower bracts of the kiekie on land; the flesh of the snapper at sea'), a Tuhoe saying that compares two prized foods.[26] *He toka hapuka ki te moana, he kaihua ki uta* ('a rock in the sea where hapuka abound, a tree where birds are snared on land'),[27] names two sources of abundant food, as does the proverb *He tutu kaka kai uta, he toka koura ki te moana* ('a parrot-snaring tree on land, a crayfish rock at sea'),[28] and the Waiapu saying *He kaka tawari ki Hikurangi, he moki ki te moana* ('a kaka feeding on tawari berries of Hikurangi is as fat as the moki fish of the ocean')[29].

Seasonal cycle

The seasonal round varied in different tribal areas, but always storage and preservation of food were key factors, whether of birds or kiore preserved by the huahua method in their own fat, or fish, fern root and berries preserved by cooking and sun drying, or the careful storage of kumara tubers. Because food might be gathered and cultivated at different locations, temporary camps were often set up, with people moving from field to forest, forest to sea, and back to the fields.

The seasonal cycle of the Ruapuke Islanders of Foveaux Strait illustrates the kind of movement that was involved for some tribes: summer was spent at home making kelp bags in which to preserve titi (muttonbird). Autumn, from March until May, was spent on the titi islands bird-catching. In winter the islanders moved to the mainland to hunt weka in June, moving further inland in August to snare forest

birds. September brought the spring lamprey season, November the time for coastal eeling, and December the shift back home again to begin making kelp bags for the new round.[30]

In the Taupo district summer was spent on the lake fishing for inanga (whitebait) and the small fish kokopu. They were caught in large numbers and dried, every village being involved day after day. In winter the tribe went to Tauhara, the bird mountain, camping there during the hunting season and preserving the birds as they were caught.[31]

Death

Throughout the seasonal cycle, ever present is a deep sense of connection with the sacred land, the receiving place of the whenua (afterbirth) which is buried in Papatuanuku, also the receiving place of the dead. As with the Celts, death was not to be feared; it was simply a passing on to the next stage, being part of the cycle of dying and becoming. Just before the grave was filled in mourners entreated the dead in farewell: *Haere ki te kopu o te whenua* ('go to the belly of the land'), to follow the whenua back to its source.[32]

The Pleiades

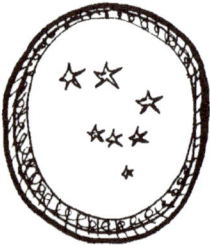

In early Polynesia there were two main seasons, based on the rising and setting of Matariki (the Pleiades), and known in Tahiti as Matarii i nia (Pleiades above; i.e. visible at sunset), and Matarii i raro (Pleiades below; i.e. not visible at sunset), corresponding to the Maori raumati (summer) and takurua (winter)[33]. This bears a striking resemblance to the Celtic observances, and it is probable that the origins for both cultures lie in South-east Asia, India or Mesopotamia where from ancient times the start of the new year was determined by the Pleiades.

In the Polynesian islands the new year began in December, with the rising of Matariki at sunset, but after the Maori came to Aotearoa there was a general change to late May or June, with the rising of Matariki at sunrise.[34] Because moon and stars were closely associated, the first new moon after the May or June appearance of Matariki marked the actual start of the year, bringing it close to winter solstice, after harvest had brought the seasonal cycle to a point of rest. The reason for the change is not known, but with the introduction of the seasonal kumara cycle it would no doubt have made sense to begin the year after harvest, as was done in so many agricultural societies throughout the world.

There were 12 months to the Maori year, but only 10 were regarded as important, with the tenth month often spanning the last two or three of the year. Ngahuru (autumn) was the name given to this time, when the crops were lifted and intense labour ceased for a while. Spring, the active and busy season, was known as Te mahuru or Te koanga, which also means 'to dig'.[35]

Stars

Stars were known as whanau marama (the light-giving ones). They were brought into the world by Tane, after he had separated his parents Rangi and Papa from their dark eternal embrace and propped up Rangi the sky with four poles. He then went to the Milky Way to find the whanau marama which he placed on the breast of Rangi the Sky Father. There they twinkle under the watchful eyes of both sun and moon.[36]

The stars were significant as the bringers of food. As the proverb states, *Nga whetu heri kai mai* ('the stars carry food hither').[37] They were the predictors of weather and controllers of the crops, first fruits often being offered to them. As in Celtic culture, they were the abode of the ancestors, and some of the ancient Maori chants tell how people have their origin in the stars and return to them at death. One myth tells how the union between the male Raumati (summer) and the female Raro (the lower world) resulted in the birth of the stars Puanga (Rigel), Takurua (Sirius) and Matariki (the Pleiades).[38]

Moon

The moon has two forms, one male and one female. Rongonui is the male form, as indicated in the name for the twenty-eighth night of the moon, Orongonui (the night of Rongo), which was one of the times for planting kumara.[39] Rongo is also the god of agriculture and peace, and his crescent, the symbol of fertility, is the whakamarama or whakaauerei on top of some of the old ko (digging sticks), used for preparing the soil for kumara planting.[40]

Hina, sister of Maui, is the female form of the moon, who as Hine-te-iwaiwa is goddess of women, childbirth and women's work, such as weaving. She has two aspects: Hina-keha (pale Hina), and Hina-uri (dark Hina), for she embraces both the light and dark phases of the moon.[41] Hina, the moon goddess, is the changing one whose phases pass through death and renewal. As dark Hina she passes out over the ocean and swims to a faraway land, out of sight, to become the wife of Tinirau, the son of Tangaroa the sea god. There she bathes in the Waiora a Tane – the life-energy of Tane, spirit of the sun – to emerge renewed as pale Hina, and thus the moon cycle of Hina begins again.[42] This beautiful imagery is reminiscent of the phases of the triple moon goddess of ancient Europe, who moves from Maiden to Mother to Crone, and is renewed again as Maiden at new moon.

The new moon, when pale Hina appeared, was an important time, greeted by the women with singing and weeping, lamenting those who had died since the previous new moon. They cried out, 'Alas! O moon! Thou has returned to life, but our departed beloved ones have not. Thou has bathed in the Waiora a Tane and had thy life renewed, but there is no such fount to restore life to our departed ones. Alas!'[43]

Another female associated with the moon is Rona, who appears as the woman-in-the-moon, much as in the European tradition there is a man-in-the-moon. Rona was captured by the moon one night after she cursed it for going behind a cloud just as she was about to fill her calabashes at a spring, causing her to trip and spill the water on the ground. She may still be seen in the moon, holding her gourds.[44]

The nights of the moon each have significance, being identified as good luck or bad luck nights for certain purposes, just as in the Celtic Coligny calendar. Each night of the moon had a name, indicating whether it was suitable for fishing, planting, or was generally auspicious or not; for example according to a Kahungunu source, whiro, the first night of the moon, was unpleasant but hoata, the third, was pleasing. The twentieth and twenty-first were seen as bad nights and the last two, the dark of moon, as bad and exceedingly bad respectively, both by the Kahungunu and the Tuhoe people.[45] A date would be fixed exactly by referring to the number of the month and the night of the moon, for example, 'on the Omutu night of the moon in the sixth [month]'.[46] Time was counted not in days of the month but in nights of the moon. Te po (night) covers the whole 24-hour period, just as 'day' does in European culture; thus someone might ask *Po hia koe ki te ara?* ('how many nights was your journey?')[47]

Sun

The sun is a half-brother to the moon, both born at the end of the ages of Te Po, their father Maku.[48] The sun wanted them to journey together but the moon did not want to be overshadowed and so told the sun to travel by day and he would travel by night. According to the South Island informant Tikao, 'the sun has more mana (power) than the moon – it is Rehua, the fire...nevertheless, the moon possesses big mana (influence) and does a lot of work.'[49] The sun was respected and the tohunga faced east when opening the school of learning and for other rituals.[50] The turning of the sun at the solstices was both recognised and named.[51]

Male and female

In rituals, men and women play separate roles, women being the first to make a sound – the karanga (invocation) – for they are the ones who give the first breath of life. High-ranking men then conduct the rest of the ritual, referring to the ancestors and the presence of death, which is tapu.

The marae (ceremonial meeting place) itself reflects these two aspects: the left side (taken from a position inside, facing out) is tapu, associated with males, death and the setting sun. The right side is noa, associated with females, life and the rising sun[52] – an interesting reversal of the European concept of right and left, where right is dominant/male, and left is passive/female. Rituals to do with life and well-being are conducted at sunrise and those to do with death and defeat at sunset.[53]

Men and women both participated in kindling fire for rituals, the woman holding the lower stick and the man moving the upper one, in an act that symbolised sexual intercourse bringing forth the spark of new life, as well as partnership between male and female forces.

The elements, the head, and other aspects

The important elements are earth, water and fire. The element air, the breath of life, pervades everything. Water is used for healing and purification; for example in the tohi ritual at the start of a child's life. Fire is even more important, being the sacred energy, the life-force of the gods. A special sacred fire known as the ahi tapu was lit at all rituals and it held the presence of the divine beings to whom the tohunga would pray.[54] The number 12 is significant[55] and the colour red sacred, to be used only for the highest ranks. The head and hair are also sacred. Fire was used to ward off evil spirits, and human hair would never be put into a fire, or else the person would die.[56]

Birds

As in Celtic society, birds are the bringers of omens and foretell the weather, night birds such as bitterns, ruru (morepork) and keruru being associated with death, sorrow and ill omens, while korimako (bellbirds) are associated with the dawn and saddlebacks with wisdom and foretelling the future. Many proverbs refer to birds as bringers of omens; for example, *Me he mea kaka haere te matuku i te po, he tau waipuke* ('if a bittern continues to cry out as it moves about at night, then a season of floods will follow'),[57] and *Ka tangi te karewarewa ki waenga o te rangi pai, ka ua apopo; ka tangi ki waenga o te rangi ua, ka paki apopo* ('if the bush-hawk cries on a fine day, it will rain on the next day; if it cries on a rainy day, it will be fine on the next day').[58] The kotuku (white heron), being white, was associated with the male, and the huia, being dark, with the female.[59] Lizards were feared and considered evil (especially the moko-kakariki, or green lizard). They entered the body, gnawing at a person's vitals, bringing illness and death.[60]

Plants

Trees and plants feature in many rituals: kawakawa leaves, konehu (kidney fern) and puawananga (clematis) symbolising death, while the mamaku tree fern with its silver underside brings peace and welcome. Harakeke (flax) leaves were used for divination and exorcism and te wao nui a Tane (the great forest of Tane) was full of atua (gods) and was tapu. Rahui (restrictions) were declared over it during the bird and rat-breeding seasons and no one could enter to take game until the rahui was lifted. Certain trees and rocks symbolise the life-force of the district and strangers entering the territory offer a piece of their hair to these sacred markers in a ceremony called uruuruwhenua.

Pakeha colonisation, with the subsequent loss of forests, fisheries and land, seriously eroded Maori traditions. This, together with urban-isation and modernisation, has resulted in many of the old food-gathering practices being abandoned; however they live on in rural areas where the traditions and rituals are safeguarded by kaitiaki (guardians) and kaumatua (elders).

1. Herm, p. 57.

2. Delaney, p. 37.

3. Stewart, p. 25.

4. Frazer, *Corn & Wild*, p. 318.

5. In the Southern Hemisphere, north and south are reversed, so that earth is the element of the south, and fire of the north.

6. Herm, p. 162.

7. MacCana, p. 48.

8. Kightly, p. 231.

9. Delaney, p. 130, and Gimbutas, p. 1 ff.

10. Delaney, p. 92

11. Stewart, p. 45.

12. Sharkey, p. 16.

13. Herm, pp. 146-147.

14. Rutherford, p. 31.

15. Anderson. pp. 73-84.

16. Davidson, p. 117.

17. Brougham, p. 39.

18. Brougham, p. 29.

19. Riley, 60-3. The saying *Te manawa nui o Whete* (Stout-hearted Whete) was a general saying for fern root, referring to the Tuhoe ancester Whete who was said to have eaten two baskets of fern root to give him energy before going into battle.

20. Banks, quoted in Davidson, p. 128.

21. Davidson, p. 128.

22. Orbell, *Poetry*, p. 84.

23. Orbell, *Poetry*, pp. 18, 19, and 84.

24. Davidson, p. 128.

25. Best, *Forest*, p. 2.

26. Best, *Forest*, p. 55.

27. Brougham, p. 44, and Best, *Forest*, p. 199.

28. Brougham, p. 44

29. Best, *Forest*, p. 193.

30. Lewis, p. 28.

31. Pomare, p. 179.

32. Salmond, *Hui*, p. 186.

33. Best, *Time*, p. 16, and *Frazer, Corn & Wild*, p. 312.

34. Best, *Time*, p. 6. In some tribal areas – the far north, the South Island and the Chathams – the dawn rising of Puanga (Rigel) in May or June marked the start of the year.

35. Best, *Time*, p. 47.

36. Best, *Aspects*, pp. 12-13.

37. Brougham, p. 110.

38. Best, *Time*, p. 49.

39. Best, *Agric*, p. 100.

40. Best, *Agric*, pp. 68 & 79 and *Time*, p. 9.

41. Best, *Astron*, p. 22.

42. Best, *Astron*, p. 28, and *Religion*, Vol 1, pp. 96-97.

43. Best, *Astron*, p. 27.

44. Best, *Astron*, p. 25. In Hawaii Rono was the name for Hina, according to Best in *Astron*, p. 24.

45. Best, *Time*, pp. 34-35, and p. 37.

46. Best, *Time*, pp. 10-11.

47. Best, *Time*, p. 28.

48. Beattie, p. 24.

49. Beattie, pp. 43-44. According to Tikao the full name of the moon is marama-huakea (moon-fullness).

50. Best, *Astron* p. 20.

51. Best, Time, p. 47, and *Astron*, p. 17.

52. Salmond, *Hui*, p. 47.

53. Orbell, *Nat World*, p. 67.

54. Makereti, p. 279.

55. Best, *Forest*, p. 293. Not only were there 12 lunar months to the year, but also 12 Po periods before humans came into existence, 12 heavens, 12 names of Io and Tane, and so on.

56. Makereti, p. 281.

57. Riley, 19-6.

58. Brougham, p. 129.

59. Orbell, *Nat World*, p. 209.

60. Orbell, *Nat World*, p. 157, Beattie, p. 94, Riley, 70-1, Mitchell, p. 259, and Lewis, p. 76.

Songs and chants for the seasons

Winter solstice

The holly and the ivy

The holly and the ivy
Now both are full well grown,
Of all the trees that are in the wood,
The holly bears the crown.

Oh the rising of the sun,
The running of the deer,
The playing of the merry organ,
Sweet singing in the choir.

The holly and the i-vy, When they are both full grown, Of all the trees that are in the wood, The holly bears the crown. Oh the rising of the su-n, The running of the deer, The playing of the merry organ, Sweet singing in the choir.

Winter solstice chant

Where is the sun in the cave of night? (repeat)
Matariki, bring us your light (repeat).

Where are the ancestors, gone from sight? (repeat)
Matariki, bring us your light (repeat).
(Rosalie Steward and Juliet Batten)

Where is the sun in the cave of night? Where is the sun in the cave of night?

Ma-ta-ri-ki bring us your light. Ma-ta-ri-ki bring us your light.

First light

Purify and heal us
Oh purify and heal us.

Pu-ri-fy a-a-nd heal us, oh-oh-oh pu-ri-fy and heal us.

Spring equinox

The kowhai and the cuckoo
Sing to my heart
And the clematis is weaving
Through the winds of spring.
(Juliet Batten)

The ko-whai and the cu-u-choo sing to my heart, And the

cle-ma-tis is wea-ving Through the winds of spring.

Summer solstice

Solstice hour
Flaming flower
See how summer dances

Ocean calls
Rise and fall
Wai korari answers.
(Rosalie Steward and Juliet Batten)

Sol-stice hour, fla-ming flower, See how summer dan-ces

Oc-ean calls, rise and fall, Wai ko-ra-ri an-swers.

Autumn

Harvest chant

Autumn is singing
Fruits she is bringing
Bounty in all of her ways
Thanks to the sowing
Thanks to the growing
Blessed the turning of day.

Harvest is holding
Season is folding
Earth time is turning around
Sweet is the flavour
Full is the savour
Gifts and blessings abound.
(Rosalie Steward and Juliet Batten)

Au-tumn is sing-ing, Fruits she is bringing, Bounty in all of her ways

Thanks to the sow-ing Thanks to the grow-ing, Blessed the turning of day.

Halloween

Halloween song

This is the night the spirits fly
This is the night the demons cry
Hey ho hi, hey ho hi,
Ghosts are flitting about the sky.

This is the night to face the crone
This is the night you're on your own
Hey ho hi, Hey ho hi,
Shadows creep and shadows moan.

Listen tonight to the baying hounds
Walk tonight through the burial grounds
Hey ho hi, hey ho hi,
Shifting shapes are homeward bound.
(Juliet Batten)

This is the night the spi-rits fly This is the night the de-mons cry

Hey ho hi-i-i hey ho hi Ghosts are flitting a-bout the sky.

General

Four elements chant

The earth the water the fire and the air
Returns returns, returns returns.

The earth the wa-ter the fire and the air, Re-turns re-turns, Re-turns re-turns.

Seasons chant

Round and round the earth is turning
Turning turning round to morning
And from morning round to night.

Round and round the earth is turn-ing, Turn-ing turn-ing round to morning

And from morning round to night.

Bibliography

Maori Background

Alpers, Anthony. *Maori Myths and Tribal Legends*. Blackwood & Janet Paul, Auckland, 1964.

Barlow, Cleve. *Tikanga Whakaaro: Key Concepts in Maori Culture*. OUP, Auckland, 1991.

Beattie, Herries. *Tikao Talks: Ka Taoka o te Ao Kohato: Treasures From the Ancient World of the Maori*. Penguin, Auckland, 1990.

Best, Elsdon.
Fishing Methods and Devices of the Maori. Government Printer, Wellington. 1986.

Forest Lore of the Maori. Government Printer, Wellington, 1977.

Maori Agriculture. Government Printer, Wellington, 1976.

Maori Religion and Mythology, Part I. Government Printer, Wellington, 1976.

Maori Religion and Mythology, Part II. Government Printer, Wellington, 1982.

Some Aspects of Maori Myth and Religion. Government Printer, Wellington, 1973.

The Astronomical Knowledge of the Maori. Government Printer, Wellington, 1986.

The Maori Division of Time. Government Printer, Wellington, 1986.

Biggs, Bruce. *Maori Marriage*. Reed, Wellington, 1960.

Brougham, Aileen, and AW Reed. *Maori Proverbs*. AH & AW Reed, Wellington, 1963.

Brougham, AE, and AW Reed. *Maori Proverbs*, revised by TS Karetu. Reed Methuen, Auckland, 1987.

Davidson, Janet. *The Prehistory of New Zealand*. Longman Paul, Auckland, 1988.

Grace, Patricia, and Robin Kahukiwa. *Wahine Toa: Women of Maori Myth*. Collins, Auckland, 1984.

Graham, Pita. *Nature Lore of the Maori*. The Bush Press, Auckland, 1993.

Haami, Bradford Joseph Teapatuoterangi Maaka. 'Cultural knowledge and traditions relating to the kiore rat in Aotearoa: a Maori perspective', E haere ana taatou ki hea?, Annual Conference of the Maori University Teachers' Association, Tamaki Makaurau, 1992.

Hiroa, Te Rangi (Sir Peter Buck). *The Coming of the Maori*. Whitcoulls, Wellington, 1987.

Ihimaera, Witi, and DS Long, eds. *Into the World of Light: An Anthology of Maori Writing*. Heinemann, Auckland, 1985.

Kelly, Leslie G. Tainui. *The Story of Hoturoa and his Descendants*. The Polynesian Society (Inc), Wellington, 1949.

Lewis, David, and Werner Forman. *The Maori: Heirs of Tane*. Orbis, London, 1982.

Macdonald, Christina. *Medicines of the Maori*. Collins, Auckland, 1975.

Makereti. *The Old-Time Maori*. New Women's Press, Auckland, 1986.

Mitchell, JH (Tiaki Hikawera Mitira). *Takitimu: A History of the Ngati Kahungunu People*. Southern Reprints, 1972.

Morrison, MF. *Matapouri then and now*. Advocate Print, Northland, undated.

Murdoch, Graeme.
  'Nga Tohu o Waitakere', *West Auckland Remembers*, ed. James Northcote-Bade, pp 9-32, West Auckland Historical Society (Inc), Auckland,1990.

  'Wai Karekare', *West Auckland Remembers,* Vol. 2, ed. James Northcote-Bade, pp 7-28, West Auckland Historical Society (Inc), Auckland, 1992.

Nahe, Hoani. Tainui Marama Whiti, Ko Te Hikurangi. The *Advertiser* Office, Thames, 1891.

Ngata, AT.
  Nga Moteatea (The Songs): A Selection of Annotated Tribal Songs of the Maori, Part IV. The Polynesian Society (Inc), Wellington, 1990.

  Nga Moteatea (The Songs), Part II. AH & AW Reed, 1961.

Orbell, Margaret.
  Trans. *Maori Folktales*. Longman Paul, Auckland, 1968.

  Maori Poetry: An Introductory Anthology. Heinemann, Auckland, 1978.

The Natural World of the Maori. Collins, Auckland, 1985.

Pere, Rangimarie Turuki. *Te Wheke : A Celebration of Infinite Wisdom*. Ao Ako Global Learning, Gisborne, 1991.

Phillips, WJ. *Maori Foodhouses and Food Stores*. Dominion Museum, Wellington, 1952.

Poignant, Roslyn. *Oceanic Mythology*. Paul Hamlyn, London, 1967.

Pomare, Hon. Sir Maui, and James Cowan. *Legends of the Maori*. Southern Reprints, 1987.

Reed, AW. *Myths and Legends of Maoriland*. AH & AW Reed, Wellington, 1961.

Riley, Murdoch. *Maori Sayings and Proverbs*. Viking Sevenseas, Paraparaumu, 1990.

Roberts, Mere.
  'Biculturalism in Conservation in Aotearoa – a case study', paper for Conference of Conservation Networks, Perth, 1994 (in press).

  'Origin, Dispersal Routes, and Geographic Distribution of Rattus exulans, with Special Reference to New Zealand', *Pacific Science*, Vol. 45, no. 2, April 1991.

  'Scientific knowledge and cultural traditions: a European view of the kiore rat', E haere ana taatou ki hea?, Annual Conference of Maori University Teachers' Association, Tamaki Makaurau, 1992.

Rountree, Katherine. *Nga Tupuna: Life in Maori Communities 1200-1769*. Longman Paul, Auckland, 1985.

Ryan, PM. *The Revised Dictionary of Modern Maori.* Heinemann, Auckland, 1987.

Salmond, Anne.
Hui: A Study of Maori Ceremonial Gatherings. Reed Methuen, Auckland, 1985.

Two Worlds. Viking, Auckland, 1991.

Simmons, David.
Maori Auckland. The Bush Press, Auckland, 1987.

Whakairo: Maori Tribal Art, OUP, Auckland, 1985.

Stirling, Eruera, and Anne Salmond. *Eruera: The Teachings of a Maori Elder,* OUP, Wellington, 1980.

Tai, Ruth. *He Taonga Whakahirahira: Treasures that Energise.* Hamilton, 1992.

Wilson, John. *From the Beginning: The Archaeology of the Maori.* Penguin Books, Auckland, 1987.

General

Anderson, William. *Green Man: The Archetype of our Oneness with the Earth.* Harper Collins, London, 1990.

Armstrong, Lucile. *A Window on Folk Dance.* Springfield Books, Ltd, 1985.

Barker, CL. *Shakespeare's Festive Comedy.* New Jersey, 1972.

Barz, Brigitte. *Festivals with Children,* Floris Books, Edinburgh, 1987.

Baxter, James K. *Autumn Testament.* Price Milburn, Wellington, 1972.

Brasch, R. *The Book of the Year: Special Days and their Meanings.* Angus & Robertson, NSW, Australia, 1991.

Bruford, Alan, ed. *The Green Man of Knowledge and other Scots traditional tales.* Aberdeen University Press, 1982.

Buday, George. *The History of the Christmas Card.* Tower Books, Detroit, 1971.

Budapest, Z. *The Holy Book of Women's Mysteries Part I.* Susan B. Anthony Coven No. 1, Ca, 1982.

Campanelli, Pauline. *Ancient Ways: Reclaiming Pagan Traditions.* Minnesota, 1991.

Cooper, JC. *The Aquarian Book of Festivals.* Aquarian Press, Northants, 1990.

Cosman, Madeleine Pelner. *Medieval Holidays and Festivals: A Calendar of Celebrations.* Judy Piatkus Ltd, London, 1981.

Cotterrell, Arthur. *The MacMillan Illustrated Encyclopedia of Myths and Legends.* New York, 1989.

Crowe, Andrew.
Native Edible Plants of New Zealand. Hodder & Stoughton, Auckland, 1990.

Which Native Tree? Penguin Books, Auckland, 1992.

Curnow, Allen, ed. *The Penguin Book of New Zealand Verse.* Middlesex, 1960.

Delaney, Frank. *The Celts.* Hodder & Stoughton, London, 1986.

Dearmer, Percy et al. *The Oxford*

Book of Carols. London, 1977.

Durdin-Robertson, Lawrence. *The Year of the Goddess: A Perpetual Calendar of Festivals*. Bycornute Books, Northants,1990.

Dunkling, Leslie. *A Dictionary of Days*. Facts on File Publications, NY, 1988.

Duggan, Anne Schley et al. *The Teaching of Folk Dance*. The Ronald Press Co, NY, 1948.

Edwards, Carolyn McVickar. *The Storyteller's Goddess*. Harper, San Francisco, 1991.

Eisler, Riane. *The Chalice and the Blade*. Unwin Paperbacks, London, 1990.

Falla, R.A, et al. Collins *Guide to the Birds of New Zealand*. HarperCollins, Auckland, 1991.

Fisher, Muriel et al. *Gardening with New Zealand Plants Shrubs and Trees*. Collins, Auckland, 1970.

Frame, Janet. *The Pocket Mirror*. Pegasus, Christchurch, 1968.

Fraser, Antonia. *The Warrior Queens: Boadicea's Chariot*. Mandarin, London, 1988.

Frazer, JG.
The Golden Bough: A Study in Magic and Religion. Macmillan, London, 1963.

Spirits of the Corn and of the Wild, Vol. 1. MacMillan, London, 1981.

Gimbutas, Marija. *The Language of the Goddess*. Harper & Row, NY, 1989.

Goodison, Lucy. *Moving Heaven and Earth: Sexuality, Spirituality & Social Change*. The Women's Press, London, 1990.

Green, Marian. *A Witch Alone*. The Aquarian Press, London, 1991.

Hardy, Thomas. *The Return of the Native*. Macmillan, London, 1958.

Harrison, Shirley. *Who is Father Christmas?* David & Charles, Newton Abbot, 1981.

Harrowven, Jean. *Origins of Festivals and Feasts*. Kaye & Ward, London, 1980.

Hawkins, Gerald S., with John White. *Stonehenge Decoded*. Publishing, NY, 1965.

Hayward, John, ed. *The Penguin Book of English Verse*. London, 1975.

Herm, Gerhard. *The Celts*. St. Martin's Press, New York, 1976.

Holden, Edith. *The Country Diary of an Edwardian Lady*. Michael Joseph Ltd, London, 1978.

Houston, Jean. *The Hero and the Goddess*. Random, NY, 1992.

Judge, Roy. *The Jack in the Green: a May Day Custom*. The Folklore Society, Cambridge, 1979.

Jung, Carl G. *Man and his Symbols*. Aldus Books, London, 1964.

Johnson, Margaret M. *Festival Europe*. Mustang Publishing Co., Memphis, 1992.

Kightly, Charles. *The Customs and Ceremonies of Britain*. Thames and Hudson, London, 1986.

Larousse Encyclopedia of Mythology. Paul Hamlyn, London, 1959.

Langstaff, Nancy & John. *The*

Christmas Revels Songbook.
David R. Goodine, Boston, 1985.

MacCana, Proinsias. *Celtic Mythology.*
Hamlyn, London, 1970.

Matthews, Caitlin.
*Mabon and the Mysteries of Britain:
an Exploration of the Mabinogion.*
Arkana, London, 1987.

*The Elements of the Celtic
Tradition.* Element Books, Dorset,
1989.

Meaden, George Terence. *The Goddess
of the Stones: the Language of the
Megaliths.* Souvenir Press, London,
1991.

Moody, TW and FX Martin, eds.
The Course of Irish History,
The Mercier Press, Cork, 1990.

Morpurgo, JE ed. *John Keats: A
Selection of his Poetry.*
Penguin Books, London, 1953.

Muir, Frank & Jamie. *A Treasury
of Christmas.* Robson Books, London,
1981.

Muir, Richard. *History from the Air.*
Michael Joseph, London, 1983.

Neumann, Erich. *The Great Mother:
An Analysis of the Archetype.*
Princeton University Press, Princeton,
1974.

Owen, AL. *The Famous Druids.*
Clarendon Press, Oxford, 1962.

Rees, Alwyn and Brinley Rees, *Celtic
Heritage,* Thames & Hudson, USA,
1989.

Rolleston, TW. *Celtic Myths and
Legends* . Avenel Books, NY, 1986.

Rosen, Mike. *Winter Festivals.*
Wayland, Hove, 1990.

Ross, Anne. *Everyday Life of the
Pagan Celts.* BT Batsford Ltd,
London, 1970.

Ross, Anne and Don Robins. *The Life
and Death of a Druid Prince.* Summit
Books, 1989.

Rowan, John. *The Horned God.*
Routledge, London, 1987.

Rutherford, Ward.
Celtic Mythology. Aquarian Press,
Northants, 1987.

The Druids: Magicians of the West.
Aquarian Press, Northants, 1978.

Sachs, Curt. *World History of the
Dance.* Allen & Unwin Ltd, London,
1938.

Seton, Gordon. *A Highland Year,*
1944.

Sharkey, John. *Celtic Mysteries.*
Thames and Hudson Ltd.,
London, 1975.

Sidgwick, JB. *Introducing Astronomy.*
Faber, London, 1961.

Sitwell, Edith, ed. *The Atlantic Book
of British and American Poetry,* Vols I
and II. Victor Gollancz Ltd, London,
1959.

Slade, Paddy. *Natural Magic: A
Seasonal Guide.* Hamlyn, London,
1990.

Slater, Herman, ed. *A Book of Pagan
Rituals.* Robert Hale, London,
1978.

Squire, Charles. *Celtic Myths and
Legends: Poetry and Romance.*
The Gresham Publishing Co., London.

Stein, Diane. *The Women's Spirituality
Book.* Llewellyn Publications,
Minnesota, 1987.

Stewart, RJ. *Celtic Gods, Celtic Goddesses.* Blandford, London, 1990.

Stone, Merlin. *The Paradise Papers.* Virago, London, 1979.

Stover, Leon E, and Bruce Craig. *Stonehenge: the Indo-European Heritage.* Nelson-Hall Inc, Chicago, 1978.

Sjoo, Monica, and Barbara Mor. *The Ancient Religion of the Great Cosmic Mother of All.* Rainbow Press, Trondheim, 1981.

The Reader's Digest Book of Christmas, Reader's Digest, 1973.

Tolstoy, Nikolai. *The Quest for Merlin.* Little, Brown and Company, Boston, 1985.

Walker, Barbara.
  The Women's Dictionary of Symbols and Sacred Objects. Harper & Row, NY 1988.

  The Women's Encyclopedia of Myths and Secrets. Harper & Row, NY 1983.

Whistler, Laurence. *The English Festivals.* Heinemann, London, 1947.

Whitlock, Ralph. *A Calendar of Country Customs.* BT Batsford Ltd, London, 1978.

Index

Adonis 83
All Saints 165
All Souls' Day 165
Antares 110, 127
Aotahi *see* Canopus
Apples 165-66
April Fool 85
Arbitration time 145
Aruhe (fern root) harvest
    77, 88, 93-94, 185-86
Attis 47, 84-85
Autumn equinox 139-53
Avebury, Wiltshire 96

Baptism 117
Barley 145
Barracouta fishing 112
Bel (Belenos) 98
Beltane 17, 96-98
Berries, edible 129, 131,
    135, 139, 140, 186
Bird hunting 159-61, 186
Bird-preserving season
    41-43
Birds as omen bringers
    65-66, 180, 192
Blodeuwedd 132-33
Blood 84, 163
Blotmonath 162
Bonfires 97, 104, 115,
    117, 133, 167-69 *see also*
    Fire symbolism
Boudica 82-83, 176-77
Boun 86, 88
Bread buried in field 150
Bride *see* First Light
Brigid (festival) *see* First
    Light
Brigid (goddess of Brigantia)
    64
Bush clearing 128

Cailleach (goddess) 63, 149,
    167, 182
Candle boats 118
Candlemas 67

Canopus 43-44, 74, 78, 93
Carman (goddess) 131
Carols 49-50, 55, 88
Castor 62, 80, 93
Caterpillars on kumara 143
Cattle, Celtic 19, 97, 162,
    178
Celtic calendar 19, 46, 114,
    145, 179
Celts 18, 97: traditions and
    cosmology 176-83
Christmas 11, 51-54, 119
Christmas cards 53
Church, the 15, 99, 117,
    119-20, 133, 165
Circle dances 55, 101, 119
Coligny calendar 179
Corn dollies 149
Corn goddesses 131,
    133-34, 150
Corn Hag 149
Corn King 120
Crone *see* Goddess
Cross, the 86
Cuckoo, 44, 100, 118-19,
    125
Cybele 84-85

Dagda 64, 132
Dead, the 37-38, 164, 165,
    166
Death 172, 188
Deer antlers 96
Demeter 17, 64, 146-48, 149
Dislocation of seasons and
    celebrations 11, 54, 119-
    20, 135
Divination 118, 165
Divine Revelation 146, 148
Dragon's net 118
Druids 182-83
Duck hunting 113, 126

Earth Goddess 131
Easter 11, 85-86
Eel catching 43, 126
Eggs 83, 87
Eleusinian Mysteries,
    greater 146-48

Eleusinian Mysteries,
    lesser 64
Eostre (Saxon goddess)
    82-83, 88
European festivals in NZ
    19-20

Faeries 95, 162, 182
Fairs 98
Feill Bhride 65
Fern root see Aruhe
Fern seed gathering 116
Fertility customs 65, 96, 98,
    134
Fir 47, 115
Fire symbolism 46-47, 56,
    64, 114 *see also* Bonfires
Fire-walking 116
Fire wheels 116
Firewood collection 43
First Fruits 125-36
First Light 60-72
First offerings 142, 160
Fishing 43, 61, 75-76,
    112-13, 126-27, 187-88
Flora (goddess) 95
Floralia (festival) 95
Flowering and sap-rise
    91-105
Fontanalia (festival) 95
Food baskets 187
Food storage and
    preservation 56, 187
Forest foods 40-43, 108-09,
    126, 129-30, 159-60, 186
Formorians 163
Fortune cookies 118
Four powers or elements
    19, 180, 192

Gardens of Adonis 84
Ghosts 162
Goddess, the 16-17, 50,
    85, 96, 132, 144, 148,
    181: as Maiden 17, 63,
    69, 102, 166; as Mother
    17, 45, 120; as Crone 17,
    131, 135, 166, 170;
    as Witch 51, 167

Grain God 131
Grain Mother 17
Great Goddess see Goddess, the
Green Knight 50
Green Man 18, 86, 88, 102
Green symbolism 47-49, 103
'Greensleeves' 102
Guy Fawkes' Day 168-69

Hakihea 109
Half Harvest festival 136
Halloween 11, 104, 165-69
Hapuku 113
Haratua 155
Harvest 131, 149-51
Harvest Thanksgiving service 151
Hawthorn blossom 100
Hazel tree 134, 165
Head, significance of 19, 182, 192
Hecate the Crone 146, 167
Hedgehog 68
Hemisphere differences 11
Herbs 115-16, 118
Hilaria (festival) 85
Hina 190
Hinau the conception tree 93
Hine-mahanga 160
Hine-mataiti 144, 156
Hine-nui-te-po 144, 171-72
Hine-raumati 40, 41, 112, 187
Hine-takurua 40, 112, 187
Hine-titama 144
Holly 48, 51
Holly King 46, 50
Honey gathering 110-11
Hongonui see First Light
Horned God 17, 102
Horo-i-rangi 161
Horus 83
Hotoke see Winter solstice
Huitanguru 140
Human sacrifice 98, 115, 163

Imbolc 63
Ishtar 83
Isis 83
Ivy 48

Kaimoana 43, 112-13
Kaka catching 41
Kakariki 157
Karengo harvest 77, 88
Kawakawa 129, 170
Keening 182
Kereru catching 41, 61
Kina harvest 77
King Arthur 145-46
Kiore hunting 155-59, 186
Koanga 80, 86
Koekoea (long-tailed cuckoo) 76
Kohitatea 125
Kopu see Venus
Kumara 80-81, 112, 129, 157: culture 184-85; harvest 141-44; pits 128, 151; planting 78-81

Labour Day 102
Lady of the Flowers 115
Lambswool (drink) 69
Lammas 133-34
Lancelot 132
Last Light 155-72
Lean Time see First Fruits
Lizards 192-93
Llew 132 see also Lugh
Lord of Misrule 50
Lord of the Grain 17
Love potions 104
Lugh (god) 131-33
Lugnasad 131-33 see also First Fruits
Lupercalia 68

Mabon 46, 145-46
Magda 131
Mahuika (goddess) 120
Mahuru-Matawai 75
Maia (goddess) 99
Maiden see Goddess
Mairehau 92

Maori calendar 18, 38, 190-91
Maori traditions and cosmology 184-93
Marae 15, 191-92
Maruaroa o te takurua see Winter solstice
Maruaroa o te raumati see Summer solstice
Matariki see Pleiades
Matiti (star) 127
Maui 120-21, 144, 171-72
May Day 97-103
May Queen and King 102-03
Maypole 85, 99, 100, 101-02
Michaelmas 149
Midsummer Night's Dream 100
Midsummer riddle 117
Midsummer's Day 114, 117
Milesians see Celts
Mistletoe 48, 54
Modron (goddess) 145
Moon 17, 86, 178-79, 189-91
Moon Hare 82-83, 86
Mother Earth 103
Muslim lunar calendar 114

Ngahuru-kai-paenga 141 see also Autumn equinox

Oak 115
Odin see Woden
Oak King 46
Oimelc 63-64
Orion 39, 62, 80
Osiris 83

Padstow Hobby Horse (festival) 97
Paengawhawha 155
Pakawera see First Light
Pan (god) 95
Pani-tinaku (kumara goddess) 79, 87, 142, 143, 144, 156

Parearau (Jupiter) 62
Parearohi (goddess) 82, 110
Partholanians 97
Persephone 64, 146, 151, 167
Pipiri 40
Pipiwharauroa (shining cuckoo) 76-77, 109-10
Planting rituals for kumara, 80-81
Pleiades 36-38, 80, 97, 177-78, 188
Plough Monday 150
Pohutukawa 108, 109-10
Pomona festival 166
Potato, planting of 93
Poututerangi 140-41
Processions 116, 164, 167
Pryderio 46
Puanga see Rigel
Puawananga (clematis) 75
Puritans and Christmas 52

Ra (sun god) 40, 112, 187
Rangiora 70
Rarawa iwi 112
Rata 126
Raupo pollen gathering 111-12
Rauroha (goddess) 62-63
Rebirth 147
Rehua (Antares) 75, 110, 120, 127, 141
Rhythm-consciousness 16-17, 18
Rigel 39-40, 63, 80, 93
Riroriro (grey warbler) 76
Ritual: definition and purpose of 9-12, 22-26; male and female roles in 191; seven stages of 24-26
Rituals: community 30-33; family 28-30; personal 27-28
Robin Hood 99, 102
Roman colonisation of Celts 13, 183
Rona 190
Rongo-maui 79

Rongomatane 78, 87, 142, 143
Rongonui 189-90
Rowan 115
Ruapuke Islanders 187-88
Ruhia 110, 127

Sacred colours 19, 23, 88, 97, 101, 182, 192
Sacred place 23-24
St Augustine 13
St Bride's Day 65
St Brigid 66-67
St John's Day 117-19
St Peter 133
St Valentine's Day 68
Samhain 18, 46, 96, 162-64
Santa Claus 53
Saturnalia 45-46
Seafood see Kaimoana
Seasons, celebration of 22-23
Seed time see Autumn equinox
Shark fishing 112
Sirius 39
Song time 145
Soul cakes 166
Spiral motif 19, 181
Spring equinox 74-89
Spring Goddess 102
Stag Lord 96
Stars 36-39, 62, 93, 127, 141, 189
Stored ripeness 171
Storytelling 182, 183
Summer solstice 108-23
Sun 44-45, 120-21, 191
Sun King 17

Tailten marriage 133
Tailtiu (goddess) 131
Takurua see Sirius
Tammuz 83, 117
Tane 104, 144
Tarata 92
Tautoru the bird-hunter 62-63, 70
Tawhaki (god) 109-10

Tawhara (kiekie) 157
Thor 46
'Threading the needle' 119
Ti (cabbage tree) harvest 77-78, 94, 128
Titoki 92, 108-09, 126
Trees, sacred 23, 47, 101, 104, 181, 193
Trickery 163, 165
Triple Goddess see Goddess
Tuahu (place of ritual) 23
Tuatha de Danann 97
Tui catching 41
Underworld 144, 146, 151, 182
Uruao (star) 127

Vega (star) 79, 141-43
Venus 62
Vegetation god 83-84, 88
Victorians and Christmas 53

War season 44
Waru 135
Wassailing 50
Water symbolism 23, 103-04, 116-17
Wearing of the green 102, 104
Weather predictions 43, 67-68, 75, 93, 134
Weka hunting 161, 187
Wells 23, 99, 181
Wha o mahuru see Spring equinox
Whakaahu see Castor
Whakaonge-kai 110
Whanui see Vega
Whiringanuku 92
Wicca 10
Winter solstice 36-58
Witches 51, 95, 166-67
Woden 48, 53
Women: Celtic 176-77; and First Light 65, 69; older 167
Word prohibitions 158, 159

Yule 11, 46-47